You will never be free

questions and answers on non-duality

Andreas Müller

Impressum

Bibliografische Information der Deutschen Nationalbibliothek:
Die Deutsche Nationalbibliothek verzeichnet diese Publikation in
der Deutschen Nationalbibliografie; detaillierte bibliografische
Daten sind im Internet über www.dnb.de abrufbar.

Copyright: 2019 Andreas Müller

Covergestaltung: Levin Sottru

Herstellung und Verlag:

BoD – Books on Demand, Norderstedt

ISBN: 9783735757357

*"**Do not follow me. I'm lost.**"*

U. G. Krishnamurti

This book contains extracts from the talks with Andreas that took place between 2017 and 2019. They are loosely sorted, but do not follow any specific order.

What	2	Surrender	40
Unio mystica	2	Let go	41
Well-being	4	Unwanted	42
What is the 'me'?	8	No presence–no absence	43
Additional realization	12	Awareness	46
The ultimate goal	14	Absolute awareness	48
Advantage–disadvantage	15	Joy	48
Innocence	16	No illusion	49
No seeing	17	Knowledge	51
Without an experience	20	Scriptures	51
For no one	21	Deep sleep	53
How to?	23	No mind	55
True self	26	No thoughts	56
Presence	27	Fear	58
Confused	30	Delusion	59
Useless	32	Clarity	60
About words	33	Non-teaching?	61
Separate setup	35	The battle	64
Complicated	36	Doership–victimhood	66
Freedom	37	Consciousness vs. self-consciousness	67
Reality	38		

Maya	68
Be here	69
No creation	70
Why	71
Shall I?	72
All is love	75
Ramana saying …	76
Koan	79
Be quiet …	80
NetiNeti	82
Stay in the 'I am'	83
Play & screen	84
Self-inquiry	86
Reincarnation	88
Make the prison nicer	89
Infant	91
The barking dog	93
Living in liberation	94
Healing & trauma	96
Lingering ideas	99
Reverberation	101
Dissociation	102
Excursions into science	104
Criticism	106
Thanks	113
About	115

The most ordinary life is unburdened by personal means. There is no person. The whole idea that you can become something better or even lose something is part of an illusion: the illusion of being 'me'. There is no such thing in the first place. Remember: I don't teach anything. There is no one.

What?

Q: What do you teach?

A: Nothing. It's all perfect already. So, there is nothing to teach.

Q: How can I see that?

A: Well, you will never really see that. When you talk about "how can I see that" you're referring to an additional state of seeing. However, perfection can't and doesn't have to be seen. It just is. In that sense, the apparent me is never interested in perfection, it's only interested in seeing it. Yet, exactly that 'me' is illusory and so would be its seeing.

Q: Do you see that perfection?

A: No, I don't. There is no 'I' thinking that I should or even could do so. Surprisingly, perfection doesn't need to see itself in order to be – it just is what naturally is.

Q: But what's its worth if I can't experience it?

A: Oh, nothing. It's not worth anything. It's not something that you own and can use. It simply is what you are.

Q: What I am? Do you mean awareness?

A: Oh, no, there is no experience of who or what you are. All there is, is what you are, but for no one. Awareness still is an experience. Nothing is having an experience of 'what is' – all there is, is 'what is'.

Unio mystica

Q: Do you think that liberation is the unio mystica?

A: The unio mystica that we speak about isn't an experience. It's neither an insight nor a knowing. It's the melting of the subject-object reality or rather the melting of the trinity of experiencer, experienced and the process of experience into no-thing; into unknowing.

Q: What's unknowing?

A: Actually, it's not just unknowing. Unknowing actually comes from not even being experienced. When I speak of unknowing, I don't refer to a personal state of not focusing on thoughts; this dizzy "I don't think" thing. Not knowing means not experiencing. Nothing can be known, because there is no experience of anything.

Q: That's the unio mystica?

A: One could say so. The interesting thing is that there actually is no such thing. Separation is an illusion, so there is no real melting back into no-thing-ness. It's not something that will happen one day. In fact, it doesn't happen.

Q: It doesn't happen?

A: No, it doesn't. This whole "union with God" thing is based on the assumption of there being a separate entity. Yet, there isn't. There is already and only union. You know, experiencing itself isn't real, therefore the assumption of a future experience is nothing but an assumption out of that illusory present experience. There is no experience now, and there will never be any experience. Seen from the apparent perspective of the 'me', liberation is assumed to be an ongoing experience of consciously knowing and feeling that everything is good. Well, not just good, really good. That ongoing future experience doesn't exist.

Q: But there are experiences of 'absolute goodness'.

A: Yes, but they are still experiences and not fulfilling at all. They never meet the longing for the unio mystica. Nothing becomes unified in that experience. It just is another experience.

Q: Hmm. But maybe it will last one day.

A: Yes, that's the hope.

Well-being

Q: What do you mean when you say that there is no bondage?

A: Both, bondage and liberation, are part of a dream – the dream of being some separate thing which is present. This "thing" lives in an apparent self-experience, which is accompanied by a sense of unfulfillment and the attempt to find an answer to that sense. That's what's called bondage. Liberation is either the idea to overcome that bondage or, how I sometimes use it, the apparent breakdown of the personal setup altogether. Seen by the person, liberation is assumed to be the overcoming of the seeking by finding something – and then become a fulfilled person. The person either wants to get rid of the seeking or it wants to get rid of itself and enter a state of liberation which, too, is assumed to exist as something in time and space. Yet, what I'm saying is that there is no person in the first place. When there is no person, there is neither someone imprisoned by what happens nor is there someone to be freed from what happens. So, the concepts of liberation and bondage only belong to the dream. Neither do you have to escape 'what is' nor do you have to bare 'what is'. It's really that simple.

Q: I don't think that it's simple. To me, it all seems very difficult. I mean, I have been struggling with this a lot for many years.

A: Yes, that's true. The 'I' is struggling with this. It's simple because it already is like that. Yet, it's impossible to do. Look, it's not just difficult to do, it's impossible! It's impossible to do, because it already is whole and complete. All experience of completeness that you create is part of the dream. All experience is illusory. 'What is' is naturally whole already, no matter what it looks like or what it feels like. And when I speak of 'what is', I don't refer to some abstract 'what is'. What I refer to is exactly this – the room, you, the feelings, the breathing, the atmosphere. That's naturally whole and doesn't need any artificial or extra state of peace or well-being. Well-being is the natural reality, we could say. Everything is totally and absolutely well in being what it is.

Q: Even pain?

A: Of course, even pain. Have you ever heard the pain complaining about itself? Have you ever heard any feeling complaining about itself? Have you ever heard any feeling of bliss uplifting itself? No, it just is what apparently happens. Apparent suffering is when there is someone who is experiencing pain and suffering. That one lives in the illusion of suffering from pain, instead of there being just pain. Fortunately, there is no one. There is neither someone in hell nor is there someone in heaven. That's the freedom.

Q: Is suffering an illusion then?

A: Well, pain is what apparently happens, but yes, the sufferer is illusory. No one suffers from anything. But feelings that the 'me' would regard as suffering may apparently happen.

Q: And then? What do you do when there is pain? Do you just sit in silence or what?

A: No, I don't. Or I may do. I don't know. Something apparently happens. Taking medicine maybe.

Q: But you just said that pain is 'it'. Why do you have to take medicine then?

A: 'I' don't take medicine, but taking medicine may be what apparently happens. And, as I said, there is no one who has to bare or accept the pain. You assume this to be a personal message with a personal standpoint. I don't see that the pain is 'it' from a personal standpoint and then can consciously react according to that state of acceptance. The pain as well as my reaction to it is what apparently happens. There just is no one there living in the illusion of doing any of it.

Q: But is that illusion wrong?

A: No, it's not. It just is what apparently happens. It's neither right nor wrong, and it's as much wholeness as everything else.

Q: But why are we working so hard to get rid of it?

A: I don't know. There is no illusion anyway, so working to get rid of the illusion is part of the illusion. Oneness does neither care nor know anything about an illusion.

Q: But aren't we talking here in order to get rid of it?

A: No, we aren't. This isn't a teaching. There is no intention on my side at least. This isn't happening for anything. In that sense, the 'me' is working on an illusory problem. There is neither a 'me' nor a 'me' illusion. There just is what apparently happens, which is exactly this and unknowable at the same time. However, it's absolutely happy to be what it is. All the complaints come from that illusory me, but even that is happily and simply itself. No one is bothered by that 'me' nor is there anyone aware of its existence.

Q: Hmm. So, all my seeking was really futile.

A: Oh, yes, there is nothing to get. The whole setup of experiencing doesn't exist. The first element of it – you – seeking in the second element – what you experience – is a dreamt reality. All results of that seeking are part of that dreamt reality as well. There is no fulfillment in there.

Q: But where can I find fulfillment then?

A: Nowhere. You can't find fulfillment. In fact, there is no such thing as fulfillment. What you're actually seeking is an experience of fulfillment. What you're seeking is an awareness of fulfillment and exactly that doesn't exist. The apparent me believes that liberation is replacing the experience of unfulfillment and seeking with an experience of fulfillment and having found. It thinks that the experience of presence is replaced by an experience of absence. However, in liberation the whole setup of experience turns out to be non-existent, but it doesn't get replaced by anything. What's left is naturally whole and full, yet there is no experience of being it. Of course, seen from the perspective of the apparent me, this can't be comprehended. All the 'me' knows – and all it exists in – is to experience, and all it has been working for its whole life is that replacement. Yet, nothing has to be seen. Nothing has to be replaced and nothing has to be experienced. This "I have to find it" is an illusion meaning that it just isn't true. Nothing can and has to be found.

Q: Well, I know that. You have said that over and over again.

A: Yes, and? What does it help?

Q: Nothing actually.

A: Yes, exactly. It's still 'you' knowing something. Yet, there is no 'you' in the first place.

Q: Hmm.

A: Yes.

Q: Can you still say something about that fulfillment?

A: As I said, what is or what apparently happens, is naturally whole and complete. It's unknowable, but by being so it's exactly what is. We don't talk about some super-reality that's all-encompassing or secretly permeating everything. It's not hidden somewhere – it's exactly this without a second, meta-reality. It is laid completely open. It's not a hidden secret, it's an open secret.

Q: Ramana said that knowing it is being it. Does that somehow fit into that?

A: Well, it could be the same what I was just saying. You can't know or rather experience it. You naturally are 'it'. Yet, the seeker will probably turn this "being it" into something that one could or should consciously do. "Being it" is the natural reality, or rather: Everything already is that. For the seeker "being it" would mean to "become and experience to be it". But that's apparently different from being it. Yes, you are it, but without having an experience of being it.

What's the 'me'?

Q: What's the 'me' actually?

A: There is no answer to that question, simply because there is no 'me' around. So, we would be talking about an illusion. There is no 'me', no soul, no presence, no self-awareness and no self-consciousness. Isn't that interesting?

Q: But why do so many teachers, religions and traditions emphasize that consciousness so much?

A: Oh, just because these are personal teachings. All the person does is to uplift its existence. All the 'me' has is its existence – that's what it consists of. And exactly that existence has to be pumped up artificially with meaning and greatness in order to make it worthy. All the 'me' knows is 'me', so 'me' must be God. (laughs). What an arrogance. An apparent arrogance, of course.

Q: Oh, wow.

A: The other thing which makes these teachings attractive is that they constantly and directly address the person. That's what the person wants and enjoys in the first place: to be seen, to be recognized as present, as existent. That's another method to confirm one's own existence. Besides that, this whole consciousness thing is referring to another state which apparently can be verified by personal inquiry and experience. 'Me' simply has to inquire and find out that it actually is pure consciousness or awareness or something like that – at least something that *is,* something that exists in some way. "To be aware of being awareness" is another of these ideas. Another thing that seems to be attractive, another promise. Personal teachings offer a state that promises salvation and fulfillment. You just have to learn to go there or to know that. "To know yourself as awareness", for example, is one of these things.

The funny and amazing thing about that is that it's completely and utterly illusory. All these states and experiences have no reality at all. It's a dreamt reality – dreamt by no one – which has no substance at all.

Q: Doesn't it have at least the reality of a dream?

A: Well, no. "There is no 'me'" actually means that there is no 'me'. So, there is no dream of 'me' either. The assumption that there is a dream that could end is already part of the dream. There is neither delusion nor a dream to wake up from. That's all spiritual dream stuff.

Q: But how can it feel so real to be 'me'?

A: If feeling to be 'me' is what apparently happens over there, it's inevitable. Then that's what apparently happens, and that *is* reality, we could say. There is still no one there though.

Q: But how can I comprehend that? How can I see that I'm not real?

A: Not at all. You can neither comprehend nor see that, just because there is no 'you'. Who would be able to do that? There is no one.

Q: Yes, but sometimes it seems as if I do see that there is no 'me'.

A: Yes, but what was the use of this? It's still someone seeing something. It's still consciousness which is conscious about some circumstance. Yet, there is neither a 'me' nor a seeing nor real circumstances. It's still trying to see and be aware of something. Exactly that's the dream.

Q: Hmm, oh, man. And I felt like improving.

A: Yes, exactly. You felt like improving. What a joke … (laughs). That's why I refer to liberation as death. It's not a seeing of something. It's not developing towards something. It's not becoming or being aware of something, whatever that something is. It just is the sudden death of the illusory experience to be that something which experiences presence. There is neither a seeing nor any other prerequisites needed. It's just dying for no reason, without having reached somewhere and without having gotten any answers. Liberation is just the end of that presence for no reason.

Q: Phew, that's really strong stuff.

A: Oh, yes, it's so different from what the apparent me thinks. It has all those ideas of high goals, holy aspirations and dreams about states of bliss and greatness. And then, suddenly, all that's left is this. All that's left is sitting in a room, being me, being you, these thoughts, these feelings. And that's the surprise: In dying nothing happens. In dying nothing dies. Nothing changes. Nothing becomes something else. It's just 'this' – for no one. There is no finding in that, no arriving, no realization, no death and no experience of something coming to an end. The whole experience of presence – me and my life – turns out to be illusory. It never existed. 'I' never was something that happened. Nothing has been born and nothing dies. There is just nothing there. What's left is this. What's left is what apparently happens. Yet, for no one.

Q: But what's 'this'? Is there an illusion now or not? Who knows all of that?

A: No one does. Who would be able to know all that? Who would be able to experience anything in the first place? 'This' isn't something that's experienced and known. It's not even something that *is*. It's no-thing for no one.

Q: But then really nothing can be known.

A: Yes, exactly. Yet, not because there is something which can't be known, but because there is nothing there in the first place. All knowing would come from that artificial awareness which experiences itself and everything else as real. Without that, who could experience anything?

Q: Wow, man. Now I see that you really speak about death.

A: Yes, seen by the 'me', it is death. It's the end of all knowing or rather the end of the illusion of knowing by the end of the illusion of experience and presence. However, 'this' is the unknown. 'Sitting in this room, being you, being me' is the unknown. Everything just is itself – without any additional experience of itself.

Q: But isn't an additional experience also itself?

A: Oh, yes, of course. The illusion of an additional experience, too, is only and utterly itself. Yet, again, for no one. The illusion of an additional experience is as unexperienced and not additional as anything else.

Additional realization

A: There is no additional realization to what's apparently happening. There is no additional insight or awareness or arrival. There is no all-encompassing love that you can consciously become. The whole setup of experiencing isn't something that exists. Self-awareness, in that sense, is nothing but an illusion. There is no self which is aware.

Q: Wouldn't you say that there is awareness?

A: Well, there is apparent awareness. Yet, there is nothing aware of there being awareness. In that respect, the function of awareness is wholeness as that, but there is no self-awareness experiencing itself as being something which is aware.

Q: Aren't you aware right now?

A: Well, who would know that, or rather: Who would experience themselves as that? There is no one.

Q: Yet, wouldn't you say that there is awareness?

A: Well, in the story, one could say that apparently there is awareness. Yet, that awareness is neither who I am nor has it any meaning. It's the arrogance of self-awareness to heighten itself and give itself importance. Yet, actually no one cares. Self-awareness doesn't have importance except within its own artificial existence. So, it's better to speak of "an illusion of importance".

Q: Hmm, okay. But why do so many teachers speak of 'awareness' or 'consciousness' as "the thing"? For them, this seems to be the highest.

A: Well, of course, seen from the perspective of the apparent me, 'me' and 'my awareness' is the most important thing. And, of course, in a personal teaching that has to be reflected.

Q: So, would you say that all of them are personal teachings?

A: At least, that's my impression. And yes, if you look at these teachings closely, you will see that most of them are actually referring to an experience of presence. Look, the 'me' realizing that it actually is pure awareness is still the 'me'. In a way, it's even right, but what's left in the end is that 'awareness is all there is', which is nothing else than saying that "all there is, is 'me'". It's wonderfully personal and wonderfully arrogant. Yet, it's just mirroring the personal experience.

Q: But they think that have found the answer. And most of them look quite happy.

A: As long as that belief works and as long as the method of coming back to awareness again and again works, the person feels wonderfully fine. It's like being successful on the path. However, it's neither free nor effortless.

Q: But some of them say that it's effortless.

A: They actually say that because as you're awareness already it doesn't need effort to be what you are. That's right in a way, yet, the effort then is to come back to yourself again and again in order not to get away from who you are with your attention and all that stuff. However, the 'pure presence' experience is just another unfulfilling experience that's transient. From there, naturally the seeking goes on and the attention naturally moves somewhere else. So, in the end, it's not effortless at all. It's just another personal game. It still comes from the impression that there is something which you are in contrast to things which you aren't. And, of course, the impression that you consciously can and have to create better circumstances, in that case to know who or what you really are.

Q: Hmm. But what's the attraction about it?

A: The attraction of that is that it promises the ultimate escape. Another part of the attraction is that you can experience it. Seen from the me's perspective, it's an undisputable experience. I mean, the experience of presence can't be questioned by itself as an experience. It can question itself as an idea, as an interesting philosophical question, yet never as an experience. So, seen by the 'me', realizing itself to be pure presence is the end of the path. It can't go deeper.

Q: Is there a 'deeper'?

A: Yes and no. It depends on how you see it. Yes, because what we talk about is what awareness is. You can neither know nor experience it, simply because there actually is no 'you' to do so. Liberation is the death of the experience of presence with the actual notion that there never was such a thing. Within the story, you could call that "going deeper". Seen from the perspective of the 'me', it's like going from presence to absence, which is nothing but death. So, no one survives that who could then arrive at a deeper level. It's the end of the illusion that there ever was someone on a path who went deeper and deeper. In that sense, it's not deeper at all. There is no "deeper and deeper". All of that is just "me and my path" stuff, which has no reality at all.

Q: Hmm.

The ultimate goal

A: Well, this message really offers nothing, however, there can also be great attraction around it. At least, we are talking about the melting of security and freedom.

Q: It sounds like the ultimate goal.

A: In a way it's the ultimate goal; however, for no one. No one will ever reach that goal, simply because it's what naturally is, what already is the case. That's the most attractive: to just 'be'.

Q: Yes, that sounds good.

A: Yet, 'just being' isn't a personal state. We don't talk about a state of beingness. You can't do 'just being'. All there is, is beingness, so you try to achieve what already is.

Q: But why is it so difficult?

A: Seen from the apparent me's perspective, it's not only difficult, it's impossible. The dilemma is that the sense of being someone automatically is accompanied by a sense of unfulfillment and mostly by a sense of restlessness. So, an experience of 'just being' is uncomfortable and feels artificial (which it is, of course, when it's "made" by the 'me'). Out of that, all 'me' knows is trying to escape that profound state – it's still a state! – into a more distracted and apparently more comfortable state. Having that experience 'me' can't even assume that doing nothing and 'just being' is so much fun. The miracle is that 'what is' is naturally whole and complete. All its problems are imagined problems.

Q: That sounds very good again. Aren't there problems?

A: Well, no real ones. Problems just are what they are, however, nothing really severe. They are just life appearing as that.

Q: Hmm.

Advantage–disadvantage

A: The illusion of there being an advantage actually is the disadvantage. The illusion that there is something which brings about fulfillment is the disadvantage – and even that's a story. Because now you might think that it's an advantage to be without that illusion. Yet, nothing is better or worse than anything else. Nothing is more or less 'what is apparently happening' and by being so, nothing is more or less whole than anything else. So, there is no advantage in anything.

Q: But isn't it better to know this?

A: No, it's not. You can't know this anyway. Knowing this is just more knowing. It's useless and unnecessary.

Q: But, don't you say this about your whole message?

A: Yes, it's useless. Seen by the 'me', which is permanently striving for an advantage, this message is absolutely useless. You see, even in me saying that there is no advantage the apparent me tries to know this in order to gain an advantage from this. Yet, exactly that's the dream.

Q: What's the dream?

A: That you're someone who is here now, being at a certain point in your life and trying to find fulfillment. Fulfillment, of course, is seen as the absolute advantage. It can only be like that, we could say, because the only possibility of the 'me' is to feel unfulfilled. That's why it's searching.

Q: Hmm, yes ...

A: All seeking, all whirling around in your personal story, analyzing things and all that stuff only takes place within that setup – the setup of being a person. Liberation isn't some finding within that setup. It's not you finding out that there is no advantage. It's not you finding out that there is no 'you'. Liberation is the complete breakdown of that setup. It's sudden, timeless and irreversible.

Innocence

Q: Andreas, what does innocence mean for you?

A: Innocence? The natural reality is innocence. Everything just innocently is what it is.

Q: But then even the 'me' and thinking about the personal story is it.

A: Yes, of course! Everything is innocently what it is. There is no right and no wrong. There is also no 'meing' as opposed to 'just being'. Everything is beingness.

Q: Wow. That sounds great.

A: Yes, nothing tries to be anything else than what it is.

No seeing

Q: I have the impression that meanwhile it's quite obvious that there is no 'me'.

A: Aha, okay. Who sees that?

Q: Hmm, I don't know. Me? (laughs)

A: You see, liberation isn't the seeing of something. Liberation isn't coming from the seeing of the circumstance 'I am' to the seeing of another circumstance called 'no me'. Liberation isn't gaining the awareness of another circumstance. 'Awareness of something' is illusory – there is neither awareness nor something to be aware of.

Q: I have heard the phrase "to be aware of being aware". What do you think about that?

A: Come on. That's another kind of a game. It's another apparent state of awareness. It sounds like this "turning the attention towards oneself" thing. However, there is no self which could shift and play around with attention. These are all personal games – not wrong, of course, yet illusory. There is absolutely nothing wrong with things being illusory. There is nothing wrong with anything. The only thing is that what's sought for within this dream – personal fulfillment – will never be reached. There just is no such thing like a person. No matter what game you're playing, it will never lead you to something beyond or to something which is more real and more 'it'.

Q: Hmm, that's not too good news, to be honest.

A: Yes, for the person, this isn't good news, but hey, who cares about the person? Only the person cares about the person. Yet, as there is no person, no one actually cares. 'This' – what is – is 'it'. That's good news. No circumstance can bring fulfillment. That's good news, too. There are no circumstances at all. That's good news. You're waiting for something to be real and for something to be really fulfilling. Maybe the next insight will be real and the search will end. Maybe the next partner will be real and will be the right one. Maybe the next guru will be real and will help me to get to a real circumstance called liberation. Forget it! Neither you – the seeker – nor any other circumstances exist. There are no real insights, nor are there real partners or real gurus. Nothing that is yet to come and nothing that has to happen 'in future'. This is timeless. This is timelessly no-thing. The assumption that you're happening right now, that's the dream. There is no happening at all.

Q: Wow, that's intense. Isn't there a way to approach this?

A: Liberation has nothing to do with any approach or coming closer. There is no approach as well as there is no becoming. There is no 'me' that is on any path.

Q: But can't there be an apparent approach?

A: Apparently, there can be the illusion of an approach. The 'me' illusion assumes itself to be on the way to wholeness all the time. "I'm moving towards the real thing" is the illusion of there being someone who is on a path towards the real thing. Yet, exactly that's the illusion. Liberation isn't the result of a successful approach. Liberation isn't the result of any development. Liberation is the complete implosion of the whole setup of seeking.

Q: But doesn't there have to be seeking?

A: Well, as I said, liberation is the end of the seeking by the apparent death of the seeker. In that death, nothing has been found, nothing has been realized and nothing has become aware. These are all illusions. Liberation is a breakdown for no reason. It's a melting away of the seeking energy for no reason and for no one. Nothing is left than what's apparently happening – and even that's for no one. In fact, there never was anything else.

Q: Why do so many teachers call it awakening or enlightenment?

A: You could call it awakening because it's like the end of a dream. The experience of being someone having a life is nothing but a dreamt reality. So, the end of that dream is like waking up. However, in the end, there is no one who wakes up as there was no one asleep in the first place. All the advice for you to wake up is personal teachings, and they basically teach how to wake up from disturbing thought-patterns. In that setup, the person can have experiences of waking up.

Q: There seems to be a thin line between waking up for someone and from someone.

A: Well, it may look like this, yet, in the story the line isn't really thin: The line is the 'me' itself. In the personal setup, the emphasis again is on the experience that the freeing feeling brings about. It feels like a gain, as if life was about that. Maybe that's even true to some degree. Yet, what the person overlooks, is that this whole life is illusory. In liberation, the breakdown of thought patterns and the according (changes in) behavior might happen as well, yet, it's neither forced to happen nor is there anyone working on it. It doesn't have any special value.

Of course, it doesn't have any special value either way, yet, for the illusory me, there is the illusion of value.

Q: Does that matter?

A: Does what matter?

Q: The whole thing that you just explained?

A: Not at all. Either way is what apparently happens. There is neither someone in liberation nor is there someone in bondage. In liberation no one is liberated and in bondage no one is imprisoned. That's liberation.

Q: Do you still want to say something about enlightenment?

A: Well, I could basically say the same things about enlightenment. Regarding that message, it's just important to say that enlightenment doesn't produce an enlightened person. The enlightenment is that there is no person in the first place. There has never been a person and there never will be a person. That's enlightening, isn't it? Or should I say "liberating"?

Q: What's the point then?

A: There is no point.

Q: You have just said it.

Without an experience

Q: Andreas, sometimes you say that there is no experience of it. How do you mean that?

A: Well, experiencing is the dream. The experience of being something is the seed of separation. It's that first sense of presence, and – bam! – you have the whole world. When there is one, you have two. When you have two, you have three, and then you have everything.

Q: Can you explain that a little bit more?

A: Well, that's the beginning of existence. That's the process of creation. The experience of presence is the birth of the 'me' – suddenly there is the first subtle something – and automatically, there has to be something around it. So, if you have one, you have two. But when there are two, there is also something that divides or connects them – a border, for example, or a bridge. That's the process of experiencing, the process of living in awareness and attention. Now you have three: the perceiver, the perception and the perceived. Out of that, the whole (illusion of a) world arises.

Q: But it's an illusion.

A: Yes, of course. There is no creation. There is no world and there is no artificial reality. That first birth – the rising of the sense of presence – did not really happen. Nothing was born and nothing became separate. There is nothing that's now present as something of its own, or rather: There is nothing that's having an experience of presence right now. Separation doesn't happen. Experiencing doesn't happen. There is no creation, and there is no illusion of creation.

For no one

Q: Can you explain a little bit more what you mean by "for no one"?

A: Well, "for no one" means that there is no additional experiencer around to experience 'what is'. There may be the illusory experience that an illusory person is having of an illusory something, however, that's 'what is', too.

Q: But it's not real?

A: Yes, it's not real. It doesn't happen.

Q: There is no experience?

A: No, there isn't.

Q: So, "for no one" refers to ... ?

A: It doesn't refer to anything. Yet, what the apparent me is looking for is an experience. All that's worthwhile for the 'me' is an experience. The statement that oneness is for no one is almost an insult for the 'me'. All that it longs for is to experience its fulfillment. It never will, though, because it's for no one.

Q: What's experiencing?

A: That's the illusion because there is no such thing. "I experience something" is the dream. In that setup, there seems to be a distance between an experiencer and what's experienced. That simply doesn't take place.

Q: How can I see that?

A: You can't. Look, what you're looking for is another experience: the experience of seeing through the illusion.

Q: That's true.

A: But there is no illusion. This 'I am' is the illusion, but as there is no real 'I am', there is no illusion either. Separation isn't real.

Q: But what shall I do with that?

A: You can't do anything with that. It's either heard or not. Both is oneness by the way, and neither way there is a 'me' involved, however, these are two apparent possibilities. Well, the "hearing" thing is a story, of course.

Q: So, it sounds like a method.

A: Yes, it may sound like one, however, it's not. One main thing about this not being a method is that there is no intention. There is no one doing it in order to create an effect for you. In fact, every effect is illusory.

Q: But you just said that maybe it's heard.

A: Which would be a story. Nothing has to be heard, of course. However, as a story, there seems to be an apparent possibility of an instantaneous understanding or obviousness of what's being spoken here. No one can do it. It's not even something real, however, the apparent me might die in that obviousness.

Q: But that's a story, too.

A: Of course, it is. Whatever I say, is a story.

Q: There is no truth?

A: No, there isn't. There isn't a real happening in the first place, so, yes, there is no truth.

How to?

Q: How to break free from the prison of consciousness?

A: There is no real consciousness. That's the outbreak.

Q: But how can I do that?

A: You can't. It's that which lives in presence which wants to escape its presence in order to be present with its absence. Forget it! There is nothing to escape from and nothing that could escape.

Q: Hmm.

A: Yes.

Q: So, there is no breaking free of anything?

A: No, there isn't. Freedom is all there is – if you like. However, for no one.

Q: There is no consciousness?

A: Well, there may be apparent consciousness, however, what you probably regard as consciousness is 'I am'. But that self-consciousness is illusory. There is no 'I am', meaning that there is no consciousness.

Q: What's liberation then?

A: Nothing really. As a story, it's the illusory death of an illusory presence.

Q: Why is it an illusory death?

A: Because the presence that dies was never really present in the first place.

Q: What can I do with this information?

A: You can do nothing with it. There is no use of any kind. Well, maybe you can become a philosophy teacher. (laughs) I'm just pointing out what already is. Regarding the apparent seeker, it's useless.

Q: But sitting here, there also seems to be a freedom around that.

A: Freedom is what already is.

Q: And peace.

A: Yes, and peace. Freedom and peace go together. This is free and whole, it's adventure and security.

Q: Wow, that sounds wonderful.

A: Yes, it is. However, for no one.

Q: Is there any resting in that?

A: No, there isn't. There is no resting in that at any level. It's that, but there is no one resting in that. There is no rest. There is also no break from that, no "falling out". It's simply all there is.

Q: But there are many teachings which say that you should rest or abide as that.

A: These are personal teachings. Who needs to or could rest or abide in anything if there is no one there to do so? No one needs to do or to be anything. It's whole already.

Q: But my experience is different.

A: That, too, is whole already.

Q: I don't get that.

A: Yes, that's wholeness, too.

Q: But I do want to get it.

A: Wholeness. You see? There is no escape. That's all what apparently happens. It's whole and free already – however, for no one. No one sees that. No one abides in that. It just is 'what is'.

Q: Hmm.

A: All there is, is 'what is' – which is no-thing as this. Timelessly there and not there.

Q: Hmm.

A: Yes, you will never get this.

Q: Did you get it?

A: No, of course not.

Q: What happened to you then?

A: Nothing happened to me. I just died. But I did not do that either. That's what apparently happened, again for no one.

True self

Q: Andreas, I'm seeking my true self. What can you say about this?

A: There is no true self.

Q: Many teachers say that one's true self is consciousness.

A: Well, 'me' can recognize itself as being consciousness, however, that's still within the story. It's still something recognizing itself to be something. That's utterly personal.

Q: Could one call that 'true self'?

A: Well, yes, in a way one could say so. Consciousness is what 'me' is. It's pure consciousness when there is no story. Then it's just pure 'I am'. Yet, it can't see that it's illusory.

Q: Why is it illusory?

A: For no reason. Everything is real and unreal – that's just how it apparently is. It's like this for no reason.

Q: 'What is' doesn't recognize itself?

A: No, it doesn't. 'What is' doesn't recognize itself to be something. It just is what it is, without any need for recognition.

Q: Any recognition is part of a story?

A: Oh, yes, absolutely. That's what I mean. Consciousness is a dream. It's not real. Why? For no reason. Can you go there? Of course not. Who could do so, when there is no one?! All this "recognizing or knowing yourself" thing takes place within a personal setup. It all takes place within an experience of presence. All 'me' knows is presence. All 'me' knows is 'me', so, by personal investigation, all it can do is to find out that all there is, is consciousness, which means nothing else than "all there is, is me". It's absolutely amazing how 'me' turns this message into an utterly personal message.

"I'm here now" is the dream. "I'm conscious of being here now" is illusory. That which experiences itself as present can't know its absence. There is no true self to be known. There isn't something that is here. That's why I say that liberation is death. It's not something that happens to someone. It's the sudden and final death of the illusion of being someone. Nothing is left. Everything is left. It's free and it's total.

Presence

A: Every experience of presence is suffering, I would say. Every experience of being something that *is* (some-thing separate as opposed to other things "out there") is naturally woebegone.

Q: But why is it like this?

A: For no real reason. As a story, one could say that it's because of the experience of separation. However, there is no real reason for it. It just is what apparently happens. Every sense of presence is accompanied by a subtle sense of unfulfillment. Out of that the seeking arises.

Q: So, what's the solution to this?

A: There is none. There is no solution to this. First, because that's just what apparently happens; secondly, because that experience of presence is illusory. It's not as real as it's experienced. Yet, that's not a solution either.

Q: Does that mean that I'm actually doomed?

A: Well, there is no 'you' that's actually doomed, yet, yes: 'Me' is apparently doomed to be 'me'. 'Me' can't become 'not-me'.

Q: So, that means to just go on seeking?

A: That's another 'me' solution, which doesn't solve anything. But yes, whenever there is an experience of presence, there will be some sort of seeking.

Q: But there is no seeking when there is no story.

A: What is then?

Q: Silence. Then there is just silence.

A: Yes, but for how long?

Q: I don't know – certainly for a while. It's supposed to be always there.

A: Yes, it's supposed to be … But are you always there?

Q: No, I'm not. But I'm practicing.

A: Look, what you're talking about is an experience of having no story for a while. However, it's transient and needs work.

Q: What work?

A: I don't know. You just said that you're practicing.

Q: Yes, it's coming back to the silence.

A: So, it's a personal thing. It's 'you' going back and forth, and it's you being aware of the one and the other. That's all in the story and has nothing to do with liberation at all. It's all about 'you' finding a way out of your misery.

Q: What do you suggest?

A: Nothing. I don't say "do that" or "don't do that". Actually, I don't know and I don't care. There is no one to be saved. All of that "I'm in the suffering and have to get out" is an illusion. I can see that this is how it's for you, however, suggesting things would just perpetuate that dream. In fact, it just doesn't happen – in the end, for no real reason.

Q: What's liberation then?

A: The end of the experience of presence as being the only reality.

Q: Hmm.

A: For no reason, of course. It's not the end of the path. It's the end of the one who assumes themself to be someone on a path.

Q: Yes, I understand. But what we really are – pure awareness – isn't on a path either. I don't understand why you say that awareness, too, is the dream.

A: "Pure awareness" is still the 'me' being aware of everything "else". 'Me' is awareness or rather: an experience of only being awareness.

Q: No, awareness is impersonal and eternal.

A: Who knows that? You're referring to an experience.

Q: But I am that.

A: Yes, right. That's what I said. This is who 'you' are – or rather: This is the experience of 'I am' – the awareness is 'what I am', and 'I' reside above or beyond everything "else". It certainly can exist without a personal story for a while. That's why it may feel impersonal. Out of that experience the conviction can arise that that's what I naturally am and if I practice enough, I can always know and experience that. It's bullshit.

Q: Why?

A: Because it's not real. There is no eternal presence. It's just an illusion. If you add the experience of time to the experience of presence, you end up with things like 'eternal' or 'always now'. Again, these are convictions coming out of the personal experience.

Q: Hmm. What's there to know then?

A: Nothing. There is nothing to know.

Q: Is there anything to be?

A: No, there isn't anything to be either. There is no you which could know or consciously be something. These would all be states and not needed at all. 'What is' and 'what's apparently happening' is effortlessly itself already. Everything happens by itself – including you. However, for no one.

Confused

Q: Andreas, I get totally confused. Is there an illusion of 'me' or isn't there an illusion of 'me'?

A: Apparently, there is one.

Q: Eh?

A: Look, 'you' don't get it. Who wants to know? There is no answer to this. There is no answer to anything. Who would be able to know it? There is no one there.

Q: So, nothing can be known?

A: Yes, exactly. Nothing can be known. There is nothing that could be known and there is no one to know.

Q: So, who knows that?

A: No one, of course.

Q: It's hilarious.

A: Yes, it is. All knowing needs a standpoint from which things are known. However, there is no standpoint. Who – or what – should know? Oneness is beautifully ignorant, simply because there is nothing else.

Q: Does it know itself?

A: Not really. It just is itself. You know (laughs), 'sitting in this room' just is perfectly itself – there is no real knowing of any kind in that. It just is what it is.

Q: So, everything just is what it is?

A: Oh, yes, absolutely.

Q: That's really simple.

A: Yes, it is.

Useless

Q: Andreas, today I noticed the uselessness of your message. I always thought that there is some use or meaning in you saying that it's useless. No, it's just useless.

A: Oh, yes, it's just fucking useless. (laughs). It only can be useless simply because it already is like this. This already is everything. There already is no 'me'. This isn't real in the first place.

Q: Oh, my God. I heard you saying this, but I still thought that this is a about something important.

A: No, it completely isn't. There is no real change. This – what is – doesn't progress towards a better 'this'. Progress is 'it', failure is 'it'. No change changes something – that's the freedom and the wholeness of it.

Q: That's really amazing.

A: Yes, it is.

Q: Now I can do anything I want.

A: Yes, you can, aside from that there is no one who could do what they want. But yes, nothing will really change anything. You will still be what you already are.

Q: That's so great to know.

A: Yes, but … you will never know that. Liberation isn't you knowing that. The apparent me might think that knowing that is the place of refuge.

Q: Ah, yes, there is no one.

A: Yes, you are what you are without having an experience of being what you are. In that sense, it's better to say that all there is, is what apparently happens. No one knows what it is, no one knows how it is and no one even knows if something is at all. Now we are back to the uselessness.

Q: (laughs).

About words

Q: I have heard you say "all there is, is no-thing" several times. Some teachers say that all there is, is awareness. Where is the difference? Aren't you sometimes a bit picky on words? Is it about the right wording?

A: No, of course, this isn't about the words. Yet, when I say that all there is, is no-thing, it's different to me than saying that all there is, is awareness. Of course, I don't know what anyone means by saying so, however, my impression is that whoever uses the word awareness exactly means that. In that way, it's just impossible for me to just say that all there is, is awareness. What I talk about is, so to speak, before awareness. What I talk about is not awareness: No-thing is what awareness is. So, awareness is not everything. Awareness is no-thing appearing to be awareness. This, too, is what apparently happens. Yet, it's not what I am. What I am is what awareness is, yet, without having an experience of being it. The experience to be awareness is another personal experience.

Q: But many teachers say that this awareness is impersonal.

A: Yes, that's right. But if you ask them where that awareness is located, they point to their body saying "it's here".

Q: Well, that's right. But some teachers even say that this awareness is everywhere.

A: Yes, so, it's still somewhere. That statement is actually coming from a conclusion. Because in the "I'm awareness" experience you even can say that awareness is everywhere. One can't say where it's not, because one is aware of all these things. So, wherever the things are, there also must be awareness. Yet, the center of awareness is still experienced as being in the body. Look, even then it's referring to the setup of experience. We haven't left it yet.

Q: Okay, what's liberation then?

A: Liberation is the end of the experience to be something that *is*; something specific. Yet, 'you' can't go there. 'You' can't do it. Liberation is an accident. It happens – apparently – or not. Nothing can bring it about, but nothing can prevent it from happening either.

Q: One more question on this awareness-thing. Why do they say that it's impersonal?

A: It may feel impersonal because it's without or detached from the personal story. For most teachers, enlightenment is when you find out that you aren't your story. And for some people this is a very intense revelation. Yet, in the end it's just another personal experience. It's going from "I am plus story" to "I am without story", but it still is 'I am'. It feels impersonal, yet, it's not (of course, it is). Usually it's not permanent anyway. That's why now you have to be aware not to get lost in your story again. (laughs).

Liberation doesn't feel impersonal. There just is no person, even if it seems to be personal. Even if there seems to be Andreas who wants this or that, there is no person behind it. The person is an illusion. It doesn't exist.

To be with a story or to be without a story – who cares? Who lives in the consciousness of there being a story or not? Who lives in the real discrimination between those two? Look, that is all personal stuff. In fact, no one cares. In fact, no one is bothered. Story or no story, personal or impersonal – it does not make a real difference. It's all 'this'.

Separate setup

Q: Andreas, can you describe the separate setup?

A: Yes and no. It's a story, by the way, because there is no such thing as a separate setup. However, seen from the person's apparent perspective, the experience is that I'm something "in here" or rather: in the body, and everything else are things out there. And all I do is living in experience, in direction, attention and focus. That's the separate setup. Seen by the 'me', that's all it knows.

Q: But?

A: But it's illusory.

Q: What do you mean by that?

A: That it doesn't exist.

Q: What do you mean by that?

A: By that I mean that it's an illusion that there is someone.

Q: But there is the experience that there is someone.

A: Apparently, yes. However, for no one. So, in the end no one knows if there is the experience of a 'me' or not.

Q: Hmm.

A: Well, the only thing that knows that there is an experience of 'me' is the 'me'. Yet, as the 'me' is illusory, the assumption that there is a 'me' is illusory, too.

Q: Is there a 'me' now or not?

A: No, of course not. It's not there.

Q: I don't get that.

A: Yes, that's true. It's not because you aren't able to get it intellectually. It simply contradicts your whole experience. The experience of the 'me' is presence. I'm saying that this presence is illusory. The attempt to understand that again comes out of that sense of presence in order to come to a real understanding. Yet, that's impossible, simply because there is no real presence.

Q: So, is there an illusion of 'me'?

A: No, there isn't. When I say that there is no 'me', this means that there is no illusion either. This is 'it' – unconditionally! There is nothing to wake up from, nothing to heal and no illusion that you have to dig through. It's simple because 'it' simply happens; it's simply what's happening.

Complicated

Q: What you talk about seems to be very complicated. I don't understand anything.

A: Actually, it's not complicated at all. There is nothing to understand. Seen by the apparent me, it all looks very complicated because that's exactly the world it assumes itself to live in: a real, complicated world that's made out of numerous parts, processes, interconnections, realities; in short: things that can – at least potentially – be known and understood. "I have to think about that and remember this and must not forget that" and so on. All of that doesn't exist. There isn't a real world made out of parts. There isn't a real world made out of things. This is undivided and literally in-different. It's one appearance, so to speak. An apparent appearance, of course.

Q: "An apparent appearance"? What the hell is that? (laughs)

A: That's what naturally is. (laughs as well)

Q: Why? (still laughing)

A: For no reason! There is no reason for it to be as it is. It's uncaused and illogical.

Q: Is there anything that isn't 'apparent'?

A: No, there isn't. There isn't some-thing. You know, what we talk about is this: sitting here, talking, being you, being me – it's utterly simple. It's already happening. It needs neither knowing nor understanding. It simply is as it is.

Q: That's wonderful actually.

A: Absolutely.

Freedom

Q: Very often we talk about freedom, but what kind of freedom is it when I don't have a choice to do what I want?

A: Yes, that's right. In that sense, there is no freedom at all. Of course, you're talking about a personal freedom. All there is, is no-thing appearing as it appears. It's free to be as it is – nothing is required for it to be as it is –, and it's absolutely bound to be as it is. There is no choice anywhere, or rather: Everything is chosen already. Of course, the apparent me would love there to be personal freedom. Either it thinks of the freedom to be able to act however it wants or it's chasing the freedom as an experience, a feeling of freedom. Liberation is neither of those.

Q: But why speak of liberation at all?

A: It's just a word. Of course, one could say that the death of 'I am' is liberation because it liberates from that sense of reality. It liberates from that neurotic drive that only exists within its artificial reality of desperate seeking. However, liberation doesn't produce a liberated entity. What's left is neither free nor bound, but just what apparently happens. One could also say that it's free and bound: 'What's happening' is free in its being unreal, and it's bound in its being real.

Q: Is 'what is' real or unreal?

A: It's real and unreal. That's why I say 'no-thing'. 'What is' isn't even an 'it'. There is no 'it'.

Q: If I could ever get that ...

A: Which 'that'? There isn't a 'that' to get. All there is, is this: sitting here together and talking – that's no-thing. It can't be gotten, because 'that' is no-thing.

Q: Is that real and unreal?

A: Yes, of course. That's all there is.

Q: That's amazing.

A: Yes, it is.

Reality

Q: What about reality?

A: Yes, that's a good question. Is there anything real? And yes, there is no answer to this. Who could ever know? Who would be there to know or experience this reality and be able to answer? Who would be there to even ask that question? So, yes, forget it. Or don't forget it. Who cares?

Q: But I think that I should know.

A: Yes, that's possible, or rather: That's what's apparently happening. It's not wrong; it's perfect wholeness in itself, however, it's a dream-like question, and all you can get is dream-like answers. It will never be known.

Q: Why will it never be known?

A: It will never be known, because there is no one to know. It's exactly that observing standpoint which is illusory. It's not real in the first place, so all conclusions that may arise out of it aren't real either. This doesn't make the urge to know wrong, it just is what it is.

Q: And what is it?

A: No-thing.

Q: But I thought that one can't know it?

A: Yes, that's right. 'What is' can't be known, that's why I call it nothing or no-thing. 'This' – sitting in a room and talking about oneness – can't be known. Try to know 'no-thing' and it will not work. It doesn't say anything.

Q: So, this whole conversation is useless?

A: Yes, it is. Of course, it is. The change that it may bring about is illusory. And useless, of course. It's whole already, it was whole already and it will be whole already.

Q: Oh, man, come on, who knows this?

A: No one knows this. Who could possibly know this? You're still dreaming of a personal realization. However, as that person is an illusion, the realization of the person must be an illusion, too.

Q: What to do then? Just live?

A: Yes, why not. The good news is that you don't have to do this. "Just living" is apparently happening already. There is no 'you' who has to or who even could do it. To live consciously is the illusion.

Q: Hmm.

Surrender

Q: Hello Andreas, I want to surrender to God.

A: Who do you think you are to think that you can surrender to God?! Surrendering to God is arrogance! Do you think that you're so big that you can even do that? Forget it. This 'I' which wants to do 'surrender to God' is an illusion. It doesn't exist. That – one could say – is true surrender: with nothing to surrender to and no one to do that. What is, is already given – apparently – exactly as it is. It doesn't need your surrender.

Q: Didn't you surrender in some way?

A: Surrender is death, we could say. It's the death of the one who thinks it could or should surrender. But it's life itself doing that. When life has enough of you, it kills you. That's liberation. It's neither a success nor something that someone does. 'Me' can't surrender, simply because it's not there.

Q: But it wants to surrender.

A: Yes and no. Yes, it wants an experience of having surrendered. It wants to surrender in order to be in a surrendered state, which is supposed to feel somehow better. However, it doesn't want to die.

Q: That's true.

A: And I don't even say that you should want to die. No, you should not. Your whole existence is nothing but a dream – there is nothing right or wrong with that. It just is what it is.

Q: What is it?

A: No one knows. There is no one there to know.

Q: No one knows 'what is'?

A: Of course not. However, it's not that there is someone who doesn't know 'what is'. There is no one there to know anything in the first place.

Q: Is it then more like a pure experiencing without a story?

A: It's not even experiencing. Experiencing is knowing – the apparent knowing that I'm something experiencing something else. Not knowing actually means not experiencing – neither a self nor something else, neither a 'here' nor a 'there'.

Q: What's wrong with experiencing?

A: Nothing is wrong with that. It just isn't real. Experiencing being not real, by the way, isn't wrong either. It all simply is what it is.

Let go

Q: Some people say that liberation is like living in a "let go".

A: Yes, it is, but not as a personal state. It's not about someone humbly letting go. "Let go" is the natural reality, so to say. Everything is loose already – an apparent playing out of what's happening. That's it. That's all there is.

Q: But can't I let go?

A: Oh, no, there is no one who could or should let go. It would be another idea of an additional personal realization. You're dreaming of an enlightened "having let go" state. Forget it, it doesn't exist.

Q: But why is it so popular?

A: Like every method, it seems to work sometimes. Sometimes, when you're busy with a problem, and letting go happens, you think that you created that wonderful experience of release. Subtly, you mistake liberation to be a more total experience of "letting go". You see? It's assumed to just be another experience. As if all your small successful 'let go's' lead to a bigger, final 'let go'. All of that is just whirling around in the dream world of the person. The experience of stress is replaced by an experience of release. Yet, it is still imprisoned in the 'me'.

Q: What is liberation then?

A: Liberation is when life let's you go. When life has enough of you and your suffering (laughs). But then it turns out that there never was someone living in a "holding on". It's all boundless already.

Q: "All"?

A: Well, there is no "all".

Unwanted

Q: When I hear you speak about there not being any experience, this sounds rather dead and boring to me instead of something that I would look forward to.

A: Oh, yes, you're right. Death doesn't look attractive to the 'me' – and seen from this apparent perspective, liberation is nothing but death. You know, what the 'me' conceives as "being alive" is the setup of experiencing. "I experience something" is to be alive. So, yes, the end of experiencing doesn't look attractive at all.

Q: Hmm, yes.

A: I don't even say that you should want it. 'Me' doesn't want to die. That's just how it is.

Q: But it wants fulfillment, or?

A: Well, it wants an experience of something that it thinks would be fulfillment.

Q: Yes, that's true.

A: All 'me' wants is to be there in order to hopefully experience fulfillment one day. Until then, the least thing that it has to do is to survive. The second important thing is to seek, otherwise it could be blamed for not having done enough. I mean, would you only count on grace? (laughs)

No presence–no absence

Q: Is there something like liberation or not?

A: Within the story there seems to be something like liberation. However, it's not really real. It's not another state that you can achieve or get. States themselves don't have any reality at all – and liberation is when this becomes obvious or rather when the illusion that life means to experience something dissolves. The strange thing is that in that dissolution it turns out that experiencing did not happen in the first place. There never was any separation. And there never was any question.

Q: So, you don't have questions anymore?

A: No, not really. There may be functional questions, however, there is no one who assumes fulfillment in the answer. When there is a seeking energy, there is an inquiry into the question in order to come to an experience of relief in finding the answer. The apparent me thinks that this moment of relief is something real and somehow permanent – and that it then took another step towards its goal of personal fulfillment. However, that's the dream. There is no personal fulfillment. It can't be, simply because there is no person. Asking questions is already 'it', yet, there is no fulfillment in getting answers. Or we could say that there is only fulfillment, in the questions as well as in the answers, but that's, of course, overlooked by the seeking energy.

Q: Why are there no answers?

A: There is no answer, because there is no real happening in the first place. Questions may happen and answers may happen. Yet, they already are what apparently happens and don't refer to a real happening.

Q: Is there a real happening at all?

A: No, there isn't.

Q: Hmm. But how can you say that?

A: Well, I can't say that, yet, that's the answer that comes out. Another way of saying it is that I died. These answers seem to come out of that apparent death. But look, it still is what apparently happens. There is nothing 'else'.

Q: Do you say that you're in a different place? Like an enlightened place?

A: No, I don't. Liberation is a no-place, so to say. There is no one who experiences himself as being something that's now here. Within the story, 'I' died.

Q: And I did not?

A: Well, that's what seems to be happening at least: 'You' stating that you're someone. On my side, there is no such statement.

Q: Didn't you say that there is no one?

A: Yes, I did, or rather that's what apparently happens. However, to be honest, it doesn't come out of an experience or awareness. Apparently, it's a "direct" answering. There is no awareness in between stating that there is a certain state that I'm in. There is no one.

Q: But don't you state that there is no one your side?

A: Well, yes and no. In a way, that's what apparently happens, however, it's not coming from an experience. Liberation isn't the awareness about there being no one. There just is no one on my side as well as there isn't on your side. When I'm referring to there being no one, I'm not referring to another state. The apparent me might assume that I'm referring to another circumstance. It experiences its presence as a real circumstance. Hearing me speak about "no-me", it might assume that I'm talking about another, somehow opposite circumstance. These two circumstances would be presence and absence. However, there is nothing present in the first place. The apparent dilemma that this presence lives in – seeking for wholeness – will not be answered by another circumstance called absence. The whole idea of presence and absence, 'me' and 'no-me' only takes place for that assumed presence. The presence of 'me' isn't a real circumstance, therefore, the absence of 'me' isn't a real circumstance either.

That's why all these religions and traditions basically fail. There is no 'me' and all this working, transcending, inquiring, trying to find and understand the 'me' is futile. It just keeps the apparent me occupied with seeking – not that it could do differently. That's what it does anyway, that's its only function, so to say. However, within that investigation it seems to have insights, to come to conclusions, to experience clarity and all that stuff. It may feel like succeeding and moving on. Yet, it is rather going in circles and never finding real answers. It's all whirling around in a dreamt reality. 'Me' will never be found. 'Me' will never be understood. 'Me' will never be killed. When

I say that 'I' died, it's a mere story. No one lived and no one lives, so who could really leave?.

Q: Hmm. But what is liberation then?

A: The death of 'me'. And a story.

Awareness

Q: Andreas, you sometimes say that there is no awareness. I don't really believe that, especially when you say that actually it's all there is.

A: Yes, okay. In a way, there is awareness, however, it's nothing. There is no experience of awareness and there is no one experiencing themself as awareness. It just is what apparently happens, however, as everything else, it's uncluttered by the experience of being that.

Q: So, is it impersonal awareness?

A: Yes, one could say so.

Q: Why do you say "one could say so"?

A: Because there still isn't something called awareness. It's still different – apparently, of course – from so-called awareness teachings, which say that you're awareness in contrast to what this awareness is aware of.

Q: Aha, okay.

A: These awareness teachings often talk about impersonal awareness, too. What they actually refer to is the experience of being awareness as the only reality while everything is just an appearance that happens *for* that awareness. This setup is just 'I am' without a personal story, which is just watching. Seen in the light of "my" message, that would still be a personal awareness which only seems to be impersonal because there is no personal story running.

Q: But that's quite often.

A: Oh, yes. That's what a lot of spirituality is about. The apparent me finds out that it's not its story but "impersonal" awareness. In a way, it's even right: 'Me' is awareness or rather: an experience of only being awareness. That's separation.

Q: But it feels good actually.

A: Yes and no. Actually, it feels good only for some time. In the beginning, it feels very relaxing because it's an apparent release from the personal story. Suddenly, there are no thoughts running about my life, my partner, my kids, my achievements and problems. Suddenly, there is silence, and I experience it. How wonderful. Yet, sooner or later – actually pretty soon, I would say – it becomes a little bit unpleasant, either boring or restless. So, the attention moves back from being awareness into the story.

Q: Is that inevitable?

A: Yes, it is. One of the spiritual ideas is that you can consciously come back out of the story to being awareness and eventually know yourself as being awareness and/or learn to abide as that. It may even seem to work for some time, however, to abide as something is a state, which needs effort.

Q: Can it become easier?

A: What?

Q: To abide as that?

A: At least, there can be the impression that it gets easier. However, all the time there has to be an 'I' doing it and experiencing it. It just is a personal thing. Apparently, of course.

Q: Why apparently?

A: It may be what happens, however, it's impersonal as well as real and unreal. That's how it is for everything that appears.

Absolute awareness

Q: So, is there something like absolute awareness?

A: No, there isn't something like absolute awareness, but there is no-thing as apparent awareness. One could call that awareness "absolute awareness" because it's not limited by a personal experience. However, it just is what apparently happens. It's unexperienced and unlocated, neither moving nor still – just as everything else.

Q: And what about the description of there being an absolute experience?

A: Well, then I would not call it an experience anymore. What is, is absolute. It's empty but not dead. In fact, it's pretty alive. I guess that's why one might call it an "absolute experience". Yet, there is no one experiencing anything, and there isn't some-thing that's experienced.

Joy

Q: What's the joy of all this?

A: The joy of all this is that the personal setup is an illusion. All of the parameters the 'me' believes itself to live in aren't real. That already is joy itself.

Q: Yes, I have the impression that for the 'me' life is a very serious thing.

A: Oh, yes, of course. For the 'me' its life, its path, its longing and its attempts to become free are utterly serious and very meaningful. Everything seems to be real.

Q: That feels very heavy.

A: 'Me' lives in the burden of reality. A spiritual teacher would suggest that you can lighten your experience by doing the right thing. In a teaching, there is always the promise that you can somehow make it. This – "my" – message doesn't suggest anything to the person, but it apparently suggests that the whole setup of being a person with all its apparent consequences is nothing but an illusion. Unraveling the illusion as illusion seems to be joyful itself. Nothing has to be found. There is no one there who is separate – that's great news, I think.

Q: But I want to get there.

A: That's the dream again. Now you're back to the teaching thing … Anyone who tries to guide you there is talking about something that you can reach. Then you're back in the personal setup, and you start running after some promise. You will not get 'life', because life isn't some-thing that you can get. This whole stuff about getting is part of the dream. It just isn't needed. Life is already the case, it doesn't have to be gotten, it always has respectively is itself.

No illusion

A: The whole idea that there is an illusion is part of the illusion. There being no 'I' actually also means that there is no illusion. You don't have to wake up from something or slowly percolate the layers of delusion. There simply is no 'I', and there is no illusion of 'I'.

Q: Does that mean that I can just live my life?

A: Living your life already happens. It's an illusion that there is a 'you' doing it and a 'you' that can lean back or whatever "from now on".

Q: Hmm.

Q: But how does this help me?

A: It doesn't – at least, not in the way in which you expect help.

Q: Why?

A: Well, the one who expects to be helped is an illusion. This doesn't mean that the 'me' exists as an illusion, no, it simply means that there is no 'me', and 'no-me' means that there isn't any illusion. All your thoughts and all your feelings are what apparently happens. They are neither only real nor are they a prison which has to be escaped from. They just are wholeness as that.

Q: But what about all these spiritual paths and teachings?

A: Well, they all refer to a person, which doesn't exist, in order to heal a separation that isn't there either.

Q: All this "working through the illusion"?

A: Yes, it's constant work; all the work apparently creates more work. 'Me' never leaves itself. So, whenever there is the illusion of 'me', there will be the illusion of there being an illusion. It's inevitable.

Q: Hmm.

Knowledge

Q: Andreas, I have heard you speak for quite a while now. Whenever I have a question, I could almost answer it myself.

A: Yes, that's true. You have heard me a lot, and now you know all the answers. "There is no one" – that's what I basically say.

Q: Yes, true. And now?

A: And now? Nothing, of course. It's useless. It's all useless. You know it all, and yet, nothing happened. It's empty. All I say is empty. You can't get anything out of it. You know it all, and you're still not satisfied. That's the 'me'. There is nothing to know, simply because there is no reality that can be known, nothing you could get hold of. That's where the concept of surrender pops in. All the knowledge did not do it. What now? Haha, there is no-where, no place to go. We could call that "surrendering".

Scriptures

Q: You know, what you have just said, I have read it over and over again in some old scriptures: "No liberation and no bondage." Now is the first time that I actually understood what's meant by that.

A: Haha, that's great. Oh, yes, it has all been out there for ages. What I'm saying isn't new. However, it's not coming from a repetition of words either. I'm not passing on any knowledge from old scriptures, but yes, it has all been said before. I'm not adding something new. There never will be something new.

Q: Isn't it new every moment?

A: No, it's not new. It may be whole – and therefore fresh. It may be unknown – and therefore adventurous. Yet, it will never be new in the sense that something will be added. What is, is timelessly ordinary and natural.

Q: Nothing happens?

A: Yes, nothing happens.

Q: It's kind of flat.

A: Without dimensions.

Q: Yes, right.

Q: You know, I think that it's amazingly different from what I thought that this is all about. This "no liberation and no bondage" thing was so abstract for me. I had no clue what this was about. It felt like some very high knowledge which I will never attain.

A: Oh, yes, that's how the natural reality feels for the 'me': Abstract. Far away. Something else that it will never reach. With the last one it's even right, but yes, what we talk about is this: sitting in a room and having this conversation. There naturally are no such things as bondage and liberation. It's so natural and "down-to-earth". Look, that's the abstraction the apparent me lives in: It abstracts itself from sitting in a room and by doing so, it abstracts itself from wholeness. By only being 'me', 'me' itself is the abstraction. Nothing else experiences itself to be separate. No chair, no room, no thought experiences itself to be something. Not even the body experiences itself to be separate. It's just the illusion of self-awareness that lives in the illusion of being something that's separate and something that's aware. It doesn't have any meeting with the natural reality, except, of course, that it, too, is the natural reality.

Q: How do you mean that?

A: Well, the illusion of being someone also is what it apparently is. It's not experienced by anyone either. In that sense, it's as unknowable and unexperienced as anything else.

Q: It's not separate?

A: No, it's not. Nothing is separate. It's not something that really happens, which could be identified as such. No one identifies the illusion as being an illusion. It, too, just is what apparently happens and it, too, just is what it is.

Q: Wow, that's really amazing.

A: Yes, it is. No way in, no way out. No movement and no standstill.

Deep sleep

Q: What happens in deep sleep? Is there a connection between liberation and deep sleep? I have heard that we are that which we are in deep sleep, and it seems as if there is a connection.

A: Yes, there is no experiencing in deep sleep. Liberation is when there is no experiencing during daytime as well. Usually, there is someone waking up in the morning. While dreaming there is usually some experiencer already.

Q: Yes, is liberation a bit like waking up from a dream at night?

A: No, not really. When there is a person, dreaming at night already is experienced by someone and so, waking up from the dreaming at night into daytime consciousness is like going from one experience to another. It already happens in presence and consciousness. In that sense, liberation seems to be closer to deep sleep in the sense that there is no experiencer at all. The dilemma is that this consciousness is a dreamt reality itself. So, liberation isn't a waking up from one state into another state;

it's the end of the illusion of self-consciousness to be something that exists. In that sense, liberation is rather like falling asleep in the evening and not waking up in the morning than waking up from night dreaming to daydreaming.

Q: What happens for you in the morning?

A: Nothing happens for me in the morning.

Q: You don't wake up?

A: No, I don't. The eyes may open and functioning may happen, yet, there isn't the experience of something additionally waking up. When there is a person, there is the illusion of something waking up in the morning. Yet, nothing wakes up. It's a dream.

Q: Is there a difference then between deep sleep and daytime?

A: No, there isn't.

Q: Is it the same then?

A: No, it isn't. There is nothing that experiences a difference between deep sleep and daytime as well as there is nothing experiencing everything to be the same thing. Nothing experiences waking up in the morning, and so, there is no break from something that was before. There is nothing there that experiences anything to be something. In that sense, there is neither deep sleep nor a state of night dreaming nor a state of day consciousness.

Q: But couldn't we say that actually all there is, is deep sleep?

A: Well, all there is, is no-thing. Because obviously, this isn't deep sleep: This is sitting in a room and having this conversation. Yet, it's as unexperienced as it's in deep sleep. This is as unknowable as deep sleep. There isn't any true statement about this.

Q: Hmm.

A: What we talk about is what deep sleep is: no-thing. No-thing appearing to be deep sleep, no-thing appearing to be night dreaming and no-thing appearing to be sitting in a room. However, there is no experience of these things to be different states. They are all timelessly no-thing. They simply don't exist.

Q: But is there no awareness anywhere?

A: There is apparent awareness. It's not real though.

Q: Some people say that there is still awareness in deep sleep.

A: Maybe, maybe not. To be honest, I have heard such statements usually during daytime, and they seemed to come out of a conclusion. No one ever reported that while they were asleep. Nevertheless, yes, liberation isn't deep sleep. And liberation isn't the statement about there still being something in deep sleep.

Q: Could one say that liberation transcends those three states?

A: Yes and no. Transcendence might be understood as another experience, yet, these states just don't exist.

No mind

Q: There are a lot of teachers who say that you have to leave the thoughts aside in order to become free.

A: Ah, yes. However, leaving the thoughts has nothing to do with liberation.

Q: They talk about no-mind.

A: Yes, that's where most teachers operate: mind and no-mind meaning thoughts or no thoughts.

Q: That's still the 'me'?

A: Yes, of course. Who is it that comes out of the thoughts? And who thinks that it's a better experience to be without thoughts that with thoughts? It's the 'me', of course, who is seeking for something. That's why you're supposed to consciously do it. By the way, usually doing it one time isn't enough, so you actually have to do it over and over again. It's a path – and that's 'me' stuff.

No thoughts

Q: Why are so many teachings about not having thoughts?

A: Well, simply because it's observed that thoughts cause feelings. As the 'me' doesn't want to have certain feelings, it thinks that in order to become free, you either have to consciously not think any thoughts or learn how to only think the right thoughts. It's working on a problem – that there are "bad feelings" – which doesn't exist. I mean there aren't really any bad feelings.

Q: There are no bad feelings?

A: No, not at all. I mean, for the experiencer there seem to be real feelings. Additionally, they seem to carry meaning. In liberation, feelings apparently happen, however, for no one.

Q: But what's the interesting thing about leaving the thoughts?

A: As I said, by leaving the story for a while, you can easily get an experience of relaxation. It's like a break from your life and your story. That can feel relaxing for a while – at least until you go back into the story. Some teachers now teach that you can learn to step out of the story again and again. However, it doesn't really work. Sooner or later you just go back into your story. And that's not wrong! All this is based on the assumption that thoughts and stories are real and therefore a real problem. You can't leave your story, simply because it doesn't exist. There is nothing there to leave from. This whole division between thoughts, feelings, the experiencer and what's going on is illusory. It's digging within and working through a divided reality which isn't divided at all. It's coming from a personal standpoint: that 'me' assumes itself to be a part, assumes thoughts and feelings to be parts and wants to find an experience of freedom within that whole happening. It's neverending. There are entire schools about this "no thoughts" idea. They are all trying to escape from 'what is' by achieving a state of personal freedom. It is always freedom from feelings, freedom from thoughts, freedom from something – for a person, of course. It's futile. It's futile and unnecessary and nothing but whirling around in a reality that doesn't exist.

Q: So, what do you suggest?

A: What I suggest? Nothing, of course. There is no suggestion. 'Me' doesn't exist. There is no one. All attempts to bring you closer to this are part of the dream. There is no 'you' that's separate – how the hell can you possibly get closer when there is no one separate in the first place!? Forget it! Your questions for advice come from an illusory standpoint asking for a solution within an illusory world. Yet, there is no 'I', and there is no personal life. Therefore, there is no advice!

Q: Hmm.

A: Yes, hmm. (laughs)

A: Liberation is an illusion. There is no such thing. There is no 'I' that's asleep and that has to wake up. There are so many courses, workshops, seminars, books, ideas and teachings out there that only support that idea that there is a person who can become something. It's such a joke.

Fear

Q: Sometimes there is great fear of dying, but sometimes I think that I also really want this. Isn't liberation also attractive for the 'me'?

A: Well, yes, it is. This energy of absoluteness and freedom is utterly attractive for the 'me'. It longs for it. Yet, the closer it comes the more it dawns on it that it will not survive there. That's its dilemma.

Q: So, what does it need to take the step?

A: Oh, no. There is no step. This whole impression of being separate is an illusion. This whole setup of being separate, of having an autonomous existence which could end is part of the dream. There is no such thing.

Q: Oh, dear. Will the illusion ever end?

A: Well, nothing ends really.

Q: What?

A: Yes, nothing ends really. There is no illusion to end either. Exactly that's the beauty: In the end, nothing happens. In the end, nothing changes and nothing needed to change. It was all just an illusion. The apparent me is awaiting something – a point of arriving, an experience of something coming to an end. It assumes liberation to be an experience of awareness about the fact that something has ended. Forget it: That's all 'me' stuff. There will never be the experience of an end. Nothing is happening in the first place.

Q: Is it like dying again and again?

A: No, it isn't. There is no one living from moment to moment, so there is no one dying again and again. What is, is timelessly what it is. There is no real movement going on and no real change. There is no step from presence to absence as this experienced presence is illusory already. Nothing is going to happen. Nothing is happening already.

Q: Are you saying that 'sitting in this room' isn't happening?

A: Yes, exactly. This isn't some-thing that's happening. It's apparently appearing.

Q: So, when you say that all there is, is this, you actually mean that all there is, is this moment?

A: No, there is no such thing as this moment. In order to have the experience of a real moment, you need to have a real awareness which is aware of there being *some thing* like a moment. But exactly this awareness doesn't exist either. This message isn't one of those "this moment" teachings. Yes, this is all there is, yet, this is no-thing. Look, you're already coming from a personal standpoint when you experience this moment. This moment is all that the apparent me has, meaning that all it has is the present experience. Yet, "I experience something" is the dream. Wholeness appearing as this dream, of course.

Delusion

Q: Is 'me' the delusion?

A: Well, in a way, it is. However, 'delusion' sounds as if there is someone deluded and could wake up from that delusion. Actually, the illusory sense of 'I am' is what apparently happens – it's neither wrong nor is someone deluded by it. Yes, it's a dream. And yes, for no one, which means that there is no one who could and should wake up from it. If 'me' is what happens, that's what happens. In fact, there is no real delusion anywhere.

Q: Hmm. My next question would be how to become free from that delusion.

A: There is no delusion. It's already part of the delusion that there is a delusion. There isn't. There is nothing to overcome and nothing to lose. There are entire spiritual groups which work on killing the 'me' or waking up from the 'me'. They all fail, basically because there is no 'me' in the first place.

Q: Spirituality is a dream?

A: Yes, it is. You know, that whole idea that something still has to happen is part of that dream – and all spirituality is about making something happen. It's all "in order to …". It's all about creating effects, taking the next step, move on towards the actual. It's all illusory; there is no one on a path.

Q: I want to come to that absolute stillness.

A: Well, it's not still either. 'What is' is neither moving nor still.

Clarity

Q: Andreas, thank you very much for your clarity. I, too, want to become that clear.

A: It's an apparent clarity. I don't have anything from it. It doesn't serve me. I'm not referring to something that still has to be realized and brought into existence. What I refer to is what's already happening. The clarity is apparent as there is nothing to be clear about. In that sense, it's utterly useless. I can't use it. Apparently, I still am as I am – as human, as touchable, as whatever I apparently am. This – 'what is' – doesn't need clarity. In fact, it's not real.

Q: Didn't your death change you?

A: Well, yes and no. Yet, not in the way the 'me' would assume it.

Q: How did you change?

A: Well, it seems that there is a tendency for old traumas and unhealthy behavior to drop off. As the person that the traumas try to protect isn't there anymore, it seems they can slowly and subtly relax and drop off. In a way, that seems to happen very organically and ordinary. Also, that doesn't seem to be a rule. What happens in that sense is neither predictable nor needed. That, namely, would be the other side: When there is no one, there is no need for anything to drop off. So, if at all, it happens wildly and freely and not as a result of conscious work on the personality. That's impossible then.

Q: Why is that impossible?

A: Because liberation is the end of the illusion that there is a conscious entity which has a life and could consciously act within that assumed life.

Q: So, you don't work on your life.

A: No, I don't. There is no one to do so.

Q: That sounds gorgeous.

A: Well, it is. However, for no one. On the other hand, it's ordinary. Gorgeousness is what naturally is.

Q: Wow.

A: Yes.

Non-teaching?

Q: Andreas, isn't your non-teaching actually another kind of teaching?

A: No, it's not. I mean, the seeker might see it like this. The seeker might assume that this is just another personal teaching providing another approach. People believe that they can decide between paths. "This weekend I will do a little bit of healing and the next evening a little bit of non-duality. And all of that will serve me." People think that they can choose between "radical non-duality" and "soft non-duality". It's really a joke.

Q: But aren't you trying to point out that there is no one?

A: That's maybe what apparently happens, however, no, I'm not trying to point out to you that there is no one. How could I do that when there actually is no one?!

Q: But it looks like that.

A: Yes, the seeker might get that impression. Yet, the seeker will have that impression anyway. Wherever the seeker believes themself to go, there is always the assumption that it happens for some reason. It may be going to the cinema, it may not be going to the cinema, it may be whatever. However, of course, that isn't a hindrance. The seeker isn't a hindrance to its apparent death, however, the apparent presence of the seeker is a hindrance to its apparent absence.

Q: Sometimes I have the impression that without these talks I would never have gone into the seeking that deeply.

A: That's funny. Sometimes people even accuse me of having invented the 'me'.

Q: Couldn't you say that?

A: No, of course not. Most people already experience themselves as someone when they come here. However, when it becomes obvious that there actually is no 'me' in the first place, they wonder why I seem to be speaking about the 'me' and its seeking.

Q: So, why are you doing that?

A: Oh, I'm not doing that – and certainly, it doesn't happen for a reason.

Q: But aren't you trying to destroy the 'me illusion'?

A: No, I don't. There is neither a 'me' nor a 'me illusion' to destroy. There is just speaking. It's wholeness as that and at the same time, it's utterly empty. In that sense, I'm not saying anything. Apparently, this sets up an energetic dynamic in which the apparent me starts to disappear, yet, that's neither intended nor seen as real.

Q: Hmm.

A: You know, it has nothing to do with understanding or us talking about how the illusion functions.

Q: That's useless?

A: Oh, completely. It's talking about something which is actually no-thing. These are stories. There is no 'me', and there is no functioning of the 'me'. If there was someone, you could just skip it all. There will never be an arriving anywhere. The assumption is that one day, you will arrive somewhere. Yet, you never will. There is neither a 'you' nor a reality that can be experienced. There are no circumstances to arrive in. In that sense, it's wonderfully hopeless.

Q: So, do you think that the 'me illusion' is something bad at all?

A: No, I don't. There is no 'me', and there is no real 'me illusion'. That's why nothing can be done about that anyway.

Q: Hmm. I always thought that you were saying that the 'me' is bad.

A: No, I'm not. It just is what it is: an apparent illusion. The word 'illusion' may have a bad reputation within the me's assumed reality, yet, that, too, takes place within an illusion.

Q: But, aren't you saying that there is no 'me'?

A: Yes, there is no 'me'. However, what apparently seems to happen is that you experience yourself as someone. It's not really happening and there is no real person behind that impression, yet, that's what apparently happens.

Q: I don't get that.

A: Of course, you don't. Who is there to get what? You would need to be real in order to really get something.

Q: Oh, dear.

A: Oh, yes. (laughs)

The battle

Q: Sometimes it feels as if there is a battle going on in me. What you speak about seems to be so obvious, but it feels as if it's not complete. I just don't completely get it.

A: Oh, yes, that's what apparently happens. This can happen when you're around that message: In a way, what this speaks about – freedom – is right in the air, yet, there still seems to be someone dancing around it. But 'you' will never win that battle. The apparent person takes on that apparent obviousness and experiences it as its own obviousness. Yet, the person will never own it. And yes, the person's experience only consists of "It's not completely obvious yet" or "I'm not completely there yet".

Q: Yes, it feels as if I have been waiting for such a long time already. As if freedom is almost graspable, and I still did not make it.

A: The person thinks that liberation is when it can call that freedom its own. However, liberation is when there is no one grasping or owning it anymore. In that sense, you will never own freedom. In liberation, you will have lost that battle and simply die (lauhgs). All that's left is freedom, which has been the case "before" as well.

Q: These aren't really good news anyway.

A: Oh, yes, these aren't good news for the 'me'. The illusion of seeking is that the experience of separation is replaced by an experience of unity. Yet, that doesn't exist. "Experience" itself means to live in separation. Liberation is the death of the illusion of separation without any replacement. The surprise is that what is, is naturally whole and doesn't need any experience of itself to be whole. It doesn't even need to experience itself as anything at all. It just is absolutely and totally itself. In that sense, liberation is just like falling asleep in the evening.

Q: What do you mean by "it's itself"?

A: There is no deeper reality that is somewhere hidden within 'what is'. Everything just naturally is itself. Nothing has a real knowledge about itself nor does anything have an experience about itself. Every chair, every tree, every feeling, every thought, everything just is purely and utterly itself. The only "thing" that seems to experience itself is the illusion of self-consciousness, of separation, of seeking. Though, even that is just purely and utterly itself.

Q: All of that happens for no one?

A: Yes, of course. In the end, it doesn't even really happen. I mean, who would be there to know anything in the first place?!

Q: What is the good news then?

A: The good news is that this battle, or rather: all of this, doesn't happen. It's what apparently happens, yet, for no one. It's wholeness as that: an apparent battling between something and nothing, which is no-thing altogether.

Doership–victimhood

Q: Andreas, with some things it seems to be quite obvious that we aren't doing them, the heartbeat, for example, or other body functions. Isn't it the same with everything else, like thoughts and actions?

A: Yes, one could say so.

Q: Why can't I see this?

A: Because it's 'you' seeing something (apparently). Look, this whole inquiry takes place within a reality that doesn't exist. There is no 'you' experiencing a separate body.

To be the watcher of things is just another personal experience. The person experiences itself as both: Sometimes it's the doer, and sometimes it's only watching. Some things can be influenced by me and others not. So, the conclusion that you have made still comes from a personal inquiry.

Q: Yes, that's right.

A: A lot of spiritual traditions point to one of these standpoints as being the path to fulfilment: One fraction says that you're the creator of everything and that you can either do anything you want or influence everything consciously. For example, some yogis want to do every action consciously – walking, breathing, thinking, feeling and so on. The other fraction says that you should just come to an observing perspective and that this will give you happiness and joy. However, these are artificial states that would have to be kept up all the time – which usually fails. It fails because these perspectives aren't real in the first place. There is neither a doer nor an experiencer. There is neither a reality to create or influence nor is there a real happening to be observed. The promise that there is one perspective which brings about fulfillment is just part of the dream, be it the observer or the creator, be it be gratitude or something else. You just can't land anywhere. Yet, doing happens, creating happens (apparently), and not doing happens as well. It all apparently happens, not leading anywhere, of course, yet, already being whole and complete. There is no one to create or observe anything or to become free. It's already free. Life is free to appear as whatever, and whatever appears is already 'it'.

Consciousness vs. self-consciousness

Q: Andreas, isn't there a function of consciousness happening?

A: Oh, yes, apparently, there is. There is apparent consciousness, and there is apparent awareness. Yet, for no one.

Q: What does that mean? You always say that there is no consciousness.

A: There isn't. The function of consciousness is what apparently happens as well as awareness and perception. However, that which seems to live in consciousness or rather that which seems to live in the experience of consciousness, awareness or perception is an illusion. In that sense, there is no one conscious of being conscious, and there is no one aware of being aware. So, consciousness may be what apparently happens, yet, it's as unknowable and unrecognized as such as everything else. It's neither important nor is it real.

Q: What about the senses?

A: Same with the senses: Hearing happens, seeing happens and so on. All this is just what apparently happens.

Q: But for no one?

A: Yes, for no one – which means that there is no additional experience of them being things that happen to someone. Self-consciousness – to be conscious of there being a self – is illusory. It's only that self-consciousness which lives in an experience to be conscious. Without that, consciousness is what apparently happens, however, it's not experienced to be something which is different from anything else. You know, consciousness isn't different from having arms or legs, for example. The difference between Andreas being conscious and a stone being unconscious just is what apparently happens.

Maya

Q: Andreas, are you familiar with the concept of 'Maya'? It's supposed to be the big illusion. Can you say something about that?

A: Well, I'm not too familiar with the concept. But if you want to use that term, one could say that 'me' is Maya. Seen from the perspective of the 'me', everything is Maya. All that 'me' knows is itself and the artificial reality of experiencing. That's what the 'me' exists of: the experience of presence and of existing as and from that separate standpoint. That's Maya.

Q: And the world?

A: There is no other Maya than the 'me'. The world isn't Maya. 'What is' isn't an illusion – the experience of it is the illusion, however, even that's a story. In that sense, there is no Maya. The assumption that there is Maya already is Maya. So, Maya is a dualistic concept. There is no Maya, and there is no illusion.

Be here

Q: So, you would say that even the simplest advice is futile?

A: Yes, of course. Some teachers even suggest simply being here. However, that's actually fucking work. That presence that they are referring to is an illusion. So, who is going to do that? Who is going to be present? It's a marvelous joke.

Q: You really teach nothing. What shall we do or talk about then?

A: Yes, I don't teach. I'm not here to teach. The whole idea that there is someone who needs to realize themself is an illusion. So, who needs advice?

Q: The apparent me does.

A: Yes, absolutely. However, there is no one.

Q: So, what about this "simply be here"?

A: Oh, nothing. As I said, that presence is illusory. To simply be here isn't that simple at all. It may sound simple – and that's exactly what it makes it interesting for the seeker. However, actually it's a great bunch of work. You never really succeed and it takes almost permanent effort to keep up that artificial state of presence.

Q: But it's helpful for a while.

A: Well, not really, I would say. You just put all your energy in being present and by doing that you withdraw your attention from your problems and the story. That may give the illusion of a successful achievement. However, it's completely illusory and takes effort. You see, it's not wrong, but it's not liberation. Liberation is effortless – there is no one left doing or not doing anything.

Q: Sometimes you say that it's "full-on".

A: Yes, everything is full-on: your daily life, habits, problems, joy, traumas … Everything is full-on 'what is'. What else should it be?

Q: Even the experiencer?

A: Well, yes, if you want so.

Q: Hmm.

No creation

Q: Sometimes you say that there is no creation. Can you please refer to that?

A: Well, there just is no creation. The whole experience of there being something that exists comes from the personal experience. It's the experience of 'I am' to be something that exists now or rather: to be something that *is* and has been created. Out of that experience arises the illusion that all that's experienced also is something that *is* and has been created. That's the experience of "me here now" and "world out there now", "I'm something that is, and this out there is also something that exists". But exactly that's the dream: that there is something that has been created or rather that there is something that has been born. Without that impression, all there is, is what apparently happens. However, there is no one who knows that or processes this information in their mind. Liberation in that sense is just the end of the artificial reality, which isn't replaced by another reality. 'What is', which is no-thing *as* what happens (and nothing *but* what happens), is naturally whole and naturally everything. Yet, there is no process of creation or experience of some-thing happening in it.
Seen by the 'me', that might sound flat – and in a way, it's flat. There are no depths in it or some hidden truth. There is no mysterious process of creation somewhere "underneath",

"behind" or "beyond" it. What is, or rather: what apparently happens, is uncreated, is nothing that came into existence. This 'sitting in a room' is unmanifest, uncreated, no-thing. It's whole and complete, not seeking for anything else.

'Sitting in a room' is happy to just be simply and completely itself. There is no additional realization of this. It's just everything. All thinking about and seeking for an additional realization in that is just whirling around in a personal story about there being a real person living in a real world needing to find real fulfillment All of that is the dream.

There is no creation. There is no real happening in time and space. Nothing ever becomes something. It's that simple.

Why?

Q: Andreas, why do you hold these talks?

A: For no reason. Actually, I don't hold them – they are what apparently happens. Well, you know, it's all out there. You can find that message over and over again, though it's more between the lines. Mostly, it's quite hard to get.

Q: Yes, but it's hard to get what you say either.

A: That's true. You will never get it. However, the words are of a stunning directness today. What we have from the past today – I mean scriptures – is very mystified and/or theologized. Like in religion, the actual message is hard to find. Today, you just say: This is 'it'. There is no one. Spirituality is an illusion. You know, it's so simple. (laughs)

Q: But for no one.

A: Yes, of course, for no one. But that doesn't matter – it's natural. There naturally is no one.

Q: Hmm.

A: Don't make a big thing out of it. There is no big thing out there. And there is nothing in here.

Q: Karl Renz said: "Be what you cannot not be".

A: That's another way of putting it, however, you can't do that either. It's what already happens. This – what's happening – just can't be different than it is. It's neither influenced nor operated by something else. There isn't something else. Nothing can be added to it nor can anything be taken away from it.

Q: What is 'it'?

A: This – what apparently happens. It's complete, and it's everything, including how you are.

Q: Hmm.

A: But there is no experience of it. There is no experience of this being complete and everything. It just is complete and everything.

Q: Is this what I am?

A: One could say so, however, there is no experience of you being that. 'You are that' means that it's utterly natural and utterly simple, but without an additional experience of 'I am that'.

Q: Aha, okay. Thank you.

Shall I?

Q: Shall I go and see gurus? When I listen to you, it sounds as if it's not needed or even a hindrance.

A: Well, there is no hindrance. There is nothing to gain, so there can't be any hindrance. If you like, the seeking itself is the hindrance. However, there is no one to stop it. The seeker can't be separated from the seeking. There is no seeker who has found or who will find.

Q: Ramana said that as long as there isn't liberation, there has to be seeking.

A: I would not say that there has to be seeking, but yes, as long as there is the illusion of being someone, there will be seeking for that assumed someone. It's as inevitable as the end of seeking when the seeker dies. In that sense, one has to seek when there is someone. The dilemma is that it sounds as if you have to seek in order to become liberated. Yet, liberation is the death of the seeker without having found anything. Liberation isn't the end of a successful seeker's career. It's the end of the seeker for no reason.

Q: So, what shall I do?

A: There is no answer to that question. Ramana might have said "be still" or "don't think about it", yet, again that's nothing that you can do. The whole question already refers to a reality that doesn't exist, namely the personal reality. When you ask "what shall I do?", you refer to someone who is supposed to be on a path towards a goal. But these things don't exist. If sitting with gurus happens, that's what happens. If that game drops, that's what happens, and if something else happens, that's what apparently happens. It's already 'it', yet, when there is someone, this will be overlooked. However, that, too, is 'it'. It can never be 'not it'.

Q: Hmm, it sounds like good news and bad news.

A: Yes, the good news is that you can't do it wrong, and the bad news is that you will not do it. The good news is that no one cares. It all is 'what apparently happens'. It's inevitable –

and exactly that's the freedom. Nothing can be different from what it is.

Q: Wow, it feels as if there is no space for me.

A: Yes, there isn't. The space that the 'me' assumes to have doesn't exist. It's an illusory realm without existence.

Q: Would you say that there is an illusion of 'me'?

A: Even that is part of the illusion: that there is an illusion. There isn't. All there is, is what apparently happens. Who would be there to know the difference between an illusion and what really happens? There is no one. And there is no illusion.

Q: But I'm trying to wake up from that dream.

A: Look, that's all part of the seeking setup. Seeking and consciousness go together, yet, they both have no reality. Trying to wake up is whirling around in an artificial reality. There is neither someone asleep nor can there be a waking up. That's the dream, however, even to call it a dream gives it too much reality. The funny thing is that it just doesn't exist.

Q: But why is it there then?

A: It's not there. The 'me', or rather the 'me' dream, isn't something that's there. It just isn't.

Q: But I do experience a self.

A: Yes, that may be what apparently happens, yet, it's not real.

Q: But how can I wake up from that?

A: You can't – simply because it's not really there. I don't even say that it has to go away. Look, you're waiting for something to happen that you can experience and know.

Q: Yes, I want this dream to end.

A: No, what you want is another experience in which the stress of life has ended. You're looking for becoming a liberated person.

Q: That's right, I guess. But, hell, I want it to stop.

A: It can't stop in the sense that you want it to stop. There is no 'it'. We always talk about an 'it' – the 'me', the seeking, the suffering – as if there were such things. But they are not 'it's'. There aren't any 'it's'. Trying to stop anything is like trying to find something. Waiting for an end is like waiting for a new beginning. Nothing will come, and nothing will end.

All is love

Q: Andreas, Ramana said that in the end everything is love. He says something like "this is where the journey ends". What do you think of that?

A: I don't know what he meant, but in terms of what I say, one could say so. Within the story, all efforts for real change or to find something more precious than 'what apparently happens' are coming from an illusory standpoint which entertains the experience of 'what apparently happens' as not being whole and complete. This could be seen as an act of violence. 'Me' is constantly saying: "Not this. Fulfillment must look different." It doesn't say this in terms of a simple idea, no; it's its whole experience. And so, it tries and tries and tries to change, to develop, to find, not noticing that it's constantly rejecting 'what is'. In liberation, this whole struggle comes to an end. In liberation, even the strongest "no-go's" turn out to be 'it'. In that sense, yes: In the end, what's left is love. Beingness is love. To not manipulate anything is love – mark you, not as a personal standpoint.

Q: But what about the seeker?

A: The seeker is love, too. This whole struggle to become one is oneness, too. It's neither logical nor can it be comprehended. In the end, even the seeking turns out to be 'it'. Even there, no change is needed.

Another reading could be that, in the end, after all those efforts, there is a kind of surrender. Liberation is surrender. Yet, it's not about 'you' surrendering. 'You surrendering' is impossible – that's 'me' stuff. Yet, surrender is death. Not trying also means no escape. What's left is what apparently happens. Strangely, surprisingly and amazingly, it's whole already. One could also call that love.

Q: What do you mean by 'it' now?

A: I mean this: being me, being you, this room, my life, your life, my problems, your problems. Every thought, every action is what apparently happens. I mean everything and yet nothing in particular. All this is love already by simply being as it is. Yet, don't forget, this love is very unromantic. It's rather ordinary. It's what already is in the most direct sense of these words.

Ramana saying "be who you are / be what you are".

Q: Andreas, Ramana said that one should "be who you are" or rather "be what you are". What do you think about that?

A: Well, the question is who should do that, or rather who needs to do that?! There is no one. You can't "do" being who you are. You already are what you are.

Q: But maybe he meant that.

A: Yes, maybe that's what he meant. We don't know. "Being who or what you are" already happens. There is no step towards that nor is there a step away from that. Yes, maybe he was pointing to that, but maybe he was just teaching – some authenticity stuff, maybe.

Q: But isn't it that I should be authentic?

A: It's the same thing. Can you be authentic when you try to be authentic? Authenticity is what naturally is. Everything just is exactly what it is. That's 100% authenticity. Even feeling unauthentic and attempting to be authentic is 100% and authentically itself.

Q: Hmm.

A: Being who you are is the natural reality. There is nothing else. If seeking is what happens, that's authentic. If the death of the seeker happens, that's authentic as well.

Q: Does that mean that 'me' can exist without a story?

A: Yes and no. There can be awareness without a story for quite a while. However, sooner or later the attention goes back into some kind of story. You know, to hang around as awareness becomes quite boring after a while; that's when you want your story back.

Q: What's wrong with the story anyway?

A: Oh, nothing is wrong with that. It's the apparent me which tries to escape into another experience. It wants to leave its life – overlooking that exactly that life is wholeness already.

Q: Well, not the personal life.

A: In a way, that too, of course. But yes, there is no personal life as such.

Q: What's it about, this "thought" thing?

A: It's a teaching that comes from personal awareness and observation. 'Me' suffers from believing its stories and the feelings that seemed to be caused from that. In order to avoid that, 'me' tries to leave the thoughts and, by doing so, avoid the so-called bad feelings. It's a technique for avoidance, like everything else the 'me' does.

Q: They call it spirituality.

A: Yes, that's what spirituality is about: finding a way out of wholeness (laughs). Of course, it fails.

Q: But again, how does it work?

A: That's the thing: It doesn't really work. Leaving the thoughts may be fun for a while, however, it actually is hard work. As I say: You have to do it over and over again. And when you have reached a moment of silence, you're supposed to abide in that … – which creates an even more artificial state. Now you have to be forcefully present in order not to allow any thoughts to happen. What a joke! Sooner or later you fail, and the thoughts are back. Funnily enough, it's all embedded into a story in the first place: that having no thoughts is better that having thoughts, and that no feelings are better than having feelings. It's all bullshit, you know. It's an idea of personal freedom. Of course, if you want to break free from your unfulfilling daily life, you have to do some of these weird techniques.

Q: It's about personal enlightenment?

A: Yes, of course. It's all about a person "doing" its experiences. And of course, there has to be something aware of it – otherwise the whole silence would be worthless.

Q: That's amazing.

A: Yes, it is. Apparently.

Koan

Q: What do you think of koans?

A: Well, in Zen, as far as I know, they are seen as some kind of method. The idea is that the master is trying to reveal some deeper truth to the aspirant. In that sense, koans are just another attempt. Of course, they may lead to the insight that they can't be understood – or even may bring about a break in the stream of thoughts followed by a moment of relaxation –, but that's about it.

Q: Haven't I heard you say that your message is a koan, too?

A: Yes, for the 'me', every sentence is like a koan. It tries to grasp, but there is no content. It's like water in the hands – it can't be kept. That's a bit like a koan, so to say. On the other, I'm not trying to reveal some deeper truth. There is no intention in it. What I say, apparently, is much more direct than the 'me' assumes it to be. The 'me' assumes a deeper meaning, which it might understand. Yet, there isn't.

Q: Yes, that's true. I'm always looking for something in the words.

A: Yes, that's the seeking. 'Me' can't hear the words, because it's looking for something in them. It can't hear the melody by looking for meaning in it. Yet, there is no meaning. I mean, that's how 'me' lives anyway. It assumes something to be out there. It's the first – the subject – looking for something in the second – an object. Both are experienced as real by actually not being real.

Q: Some teachers suggest bringing one's attention back to the subject.

A: It's the same thing actually: moving the attention towards something. Here, "the subject" is objectified. All that's being done here is to create a temporary experience. It may be an experience of silence and calmness, however, it's temporary.

Q: But some people say that it's eternal.

A: That's right. But it actually is a conclusion. Because whenever it's done, there is the experience of that silence and calmness, so the conclusion is that it must always be there. Yet, the actual experience is temporary, simply because the attention apparently moves on to another "object".

Q: Can't I learn to stay there?

A: No, not really, that's what I just said: The attention naturally moves away from just being present, simply because 'being present' is just another unfulfilling state. So, to remain as presence becomes another impossible task. However, there may be the illusion of success because the conviction of being that calm presence may increase. The dilemma is that it's accompanied by the permanent effort and has no connection with what I would call liberation.

Q: Is liberation effortless?

A: Yes, of course! It's effortless, or rather: There is no liberation, but the sense of effort is part of the illusion. Without illusion, there is no effort. It's as simple as that.

Q: Do you never get stressed?

A: I do get stressed – apparently, effortlessly, of course. However, the idea that 'being stressed' has to be transformed through personal effort into something more holy or whatever, doesn't arise in liberation. So, yes, apparent effort within the apparent daily life may apparently happen. (laughs)

Be quiet – before your birth

Q: Papaji said "be quiet". What do you think about that?

A: In a non-dual sense, "be quiet" would mean "remain before you were born". However, there is no one who could do that, insofar it's just another story. There is no 'me' there before the apparent arising of the 'me' illusion which could prevent that from happening.

Q: So, the me also happens by itself?

A: Yes, of course. It doesn't really happen anyway, however, no one is having a 'me' and could get rid of it. There just is no one.

Q: But why are there all those teachings?

A: I have no idea. There is no one and there is no choice anywhere. The birth of 'me' is like waking up in the morning: No one does that. There simply is no one there before the waking up happens who could prevent it from happening. That's the apparent birth of 'me' – the birth of awareness meaning the birth of the sense of presence. No one can prevent it from happening and actually, no one has to. The assumption that the apparent birth of that illusion should not happen is part of the dream of 'me'. Yet, there is nothing wrong with it.

Q: Well, that's what you say.

A: Oh, yes, of course, it still is what it apparently is: an illusion without any reality.

Q: What do you mean by that?

A: I mean that there is no such thing. There is neither a 'me' nor a sense of presence nor an illusion. There is nothing to get rid of. Nothing has been born forty years ago, nothing woke up in the morning, nothing is here right now, nothing will go to sleep and nothing will die. That whole existence doesn't exist.

Q: But how can you know that?

A: I can't. I don't know that. There is no one.

Q: So, when Papaji said "be quiet", what did he mean?

A: I have no idea. Seeing this statement in the eyes of this message, it must have meant "don't get born". Yet, maybe it was just another pointing, however, no one is able to do that, simply because there is no one. It's the same turn-out like the 'me' thinking that it has to consciously become 'no me'. Who would be able to do that? There is no one. Yet, my impression is that most of Papaji's disciples think that "be quiet" meant not to think. If that was his message, it had nothing in common with what I say. All this "no thoughts" thing is rather superficial and not really getting the point.

Q: What is the point then?

A: There is no point.

Q: You have just said it.

A: Yes, I'm sorry, yet, there is no point. In a teaching, there is always a point. It's always about something – something that's right or worthwhile and something that's wrong or neglectable. Being with thoughts is worse than being without thoughts. I mean, who could be aware of that anyway? Who could be there to suffer from there being thoughts, and who would be there to enjoy the silence? There is no one. Awareness and all these states that seem to happen within awareness aren't real. They don't exist. There is no separate awareness that's aware of a separate happening. The apparent melting of that setup leaves nothing behind than apparent blankness. Empty fullness for no one.

NetiNeti

Q: Is what you do "NetiNeti"?

A: Well, yes and no. It's naturally "NetiNeti" but not a method called "NetiNeti". It's not "NetiNeti" in order to go somewhere. It's just a natural and direct answering. 'Me' is asking "Is 'what is' awareness?", and the answer is "no". It asks "Is enlightenment a state of happiness?", and the answer is "no". That's "NetiNeti" – simple and natural. Used as a method, it's just another game the 'me' plays. It's a fake producing fake results. In fact, the answer isn't even "no". There is no real answer. Because all that's negated doesn't exist anyway. I'm just saying "no" to what's not in the first place – 'me', enlightenment, states and all that stuff. "NetiNeti" also implies an unspoken confirmation of 'what is'. So, "not this" is just one half of the coin because everything "is it", too. So, the answer always is "yes and no", which, in fact, is no answer at all. That's "NetiNeti". This whole event is naturally "NetiNeti".

Stay in the 'I am'

Q: Andreas, have you heard about Nisargadatta Maharaj? He suggested staying in the 'I am', which might support the death of the 'me'.

A: It's a good idea, however, it's not working. (laughs)

Q: Why is it a teaching?

A: It's a teaching because it addresses a person that's supposed to be able to consciously do something and take a position. Yet, there is no one. 'I am' is an illusion, and to stay in the 'I am' in order to go beyond the 'I am' is just futile. It's self-confirming, which is the only interest of the self. The interesting thing is that Nisargadatta himself renounced it one or two years before he died. In one of his last books his mentioned that the most important thing was not mentioned in his "I am that" books. As I said, conceptually, 'I am' sounds like a good idea: To rest as pure presence seems to be a closer place to the border to absence than when you're caught in a personal story.

Q: But that sounds good.

A: Yes, but it's a story. Theoretically, you could die right out of your personal story. Why not?! Yet, there is no one anyway: First, there is no one to choose an inner position. Secondly, there are no real circumstances. And thirdly, this message completely addresses an artificial reality. Nisargadatta must have noticed it because he did mention it at the end of his life. He could not keep it up, because there actually is no one.

Q: So, would you say that he was coming from a different perspective?

A: Well, who knows. Yet, his famous books "I am that" are clearly teachings, simply overlooking that there actually is no one. Of course, one could say that awareness – or the pure 'I am' state – is closer to absence, however, it's just a damn theory. And as I said, it's still assuming there to be someone who can do something in order to raise the chance to become something else. This is nothing else than a usual personal teaching. It addresses someone in order to xyz ... In the end, he himself admitted that it was a teaching. Funnily enough, the "I am that" books are the most popular books from Nisargadatta amongst seekers. Of course, because it's a teaching and keeps the search going.

Play & screen

Q: Andreas, do you know the picture that some teachers use, which is the picture of the screen and the movie on the screen? They say that often we are lost in the movie and forget that we are actually the screen.

A: Yes, I know that picture. Yet, what this picture refers to is an awareness teaching. It actually perfectly describes the personal experience where 'I am the screen' – which is the awareness – and everything happens within my awareness. By personal inquiry, 'me' can understand that it's different from what it's aware of. As a way to escape the seeking in the so-called outside world, you're supposed to understand that you're that awareness. Of course, and that's where the teaching sets in, you have to consciously do so. Usually, it's about shifting the attention from the outside to the inside. The attempt is to come from an experience of movement to an experience of resting. The promise within that is that, by doing so, you can become free from the burden and the entanglements of daily life.

Q: So, what do you say?

A: I don't say anything.

Q: But what would you do with that?

A: Well, you're neither the awareness nor what you're aware of. Or you're both the awareness as well as what you're aware of. It doesn't matter, simply because every experience of being something is illusory. You're again trying to squeeze in 'me'. Yet, there is no one. There is not something which you are, or rather there isn't an experience of what you are. You see, this whole picture of a screen points to a dual setup. The actual experience is duality.

Q: But the movie and the screen are 'not-two'.

A: Yes, that's what they say, yet, it's coming from an understanding and a concept. Of course, you can say so. However, in their actual experience, or rather what the teaching exactly points to in my opinion, is that you are the one thing, namely the awareness, and not the other thing, namely the happening on the screen. That's what the whole teaching is based on: separation and duality. It's the attempt to find liberation and peace in one single experience. Good luck.

Q: Is that bad?

A: No, of course, it's not. It just has nothing to do with what we talk about today. There is just no connection to what I would call liberation.

Q: They say that this awareness is divine.

A: Oh, yes, of course. It's the highest of the highest and the purest of the purest – and all that stuff. It's permanently saying "I am all that is", "I am all that is", … It's the absolute self-heightening of 'me'. I mean, all 'me' knows is 'me', so naturally, all results of the me's inquiry of its existence must lead to that result: "I am". Isn't that great? (laughs)

Q: There really is no way out.

A: No, there isn't. That there has to be one, is the dream.

Self-inquiry

Q: Who are you? Who am I? Is there a way to find an answer to that?

A: No, there isn't.

Q: Can't I self-inquire?

A: No, not really. Who wants to inquire? Who wants to come to conclusions and know? There is no one. It's all the 'me', which has no reality at all.

Q: But I do want to know the reality.

A: It's unknowable. What is, is no-thing. The one who wants to know that is an illusion.

Q: But I can …

A: Who is that 'I'?

Q: But when I ask myself …

A: Who is that 'I'? It doesn't exist!

Q: But I can see that there is no 'I'.

A: Again that's me knowing something. It's an illusory knowing of an illusory person. Forget it, it's not worth anything.

Q: It helps me to calm down sometimes.

A: Oh, yes, that's what it does: help. Who is that wimp which needs help?! It's a total illusion. All of that is the 'me'. 'Me' is trying to know something in order to change its experience. If it works, it feels like a success, in short: "I have been helped." It's all within 'me'.

Q: Is it wrong?

A: No, it isn't. It just is what it apparently is: 'me' stuff.

Q: What should I do with that?

A: Oh, nothing. That's what apparently happens. No one should or could do anything with it. It's no-thing.

Q: Am I not supposed to leave the "I" dream behind?

A: Oh, no. Again: Who would or could do so? The assumption that there is a real "I" dream running already is part of the dream. "There is no 'I'" means that there is no dream either. That there is an 'I' is an illusion, meaning that there is neither an 'I' nor an illusion. It simply is as it is – for no one.

Q: Hmm ...

A: That's the beauty of that message: There is nowhere to go, no step to take. There isn't anyone here needing to do so. This is utter brilliance, however, for no one.

Q: But who knows that?

A: No one does. Oneness seems to see everything – actually it's everything – and yet, remains completely blind. It's wonderfully ignorant by not recognizing anything that's not it – even the illusion of being a person. Oneness doesn't recognize 'me' as such. 'It' just is it.

Reincarnation

Q: When I hear you speak, I assume that you don't think much of the idea of reincarnation, right?

A: Well, yes, there is no incarnation, so there is no reincarnation either.

Q: Hmm. So, can I be sure that with my death it's all over?

A: Well, yes and no. Nothing can be known really. Who would know whether something ends or whether something goes on? The dilemma is that this message and the realm where your question takes place in never really meet. Your question takes place within a reality that doesn't really exist. As I said, there isn't even one incarnation. This means that there will not be a real death to that one incarnation either. Exactly that death would be what you have asked for: "Does it end when the body dies?" Yes, when the body dies, that's what apparently happens. At least, it will be the end of that body and the end of the function of awareness and consciousness. Nothing else can be known.

Q: Where does this concept of reincarnation come from?

A: In a way, it comes from the person's experience. The person experiences a coming and going every day, respectively every night. It's actually easy to think of death as a long night. If you like, you can put the whole concept of reincarnation within the experience of one lifespan. Since the day that you were born – the day when self-awareness arose – you experience a coming and a going, a rise of self-awareness and a vanishing of that. Together with it, the world with all its problems arises and with the vanishing of it, the world with all its problems vanishes, too. However, for no one. The thing is that this dance – the dance between presence and absence – is what apparently happens. There is neither a real presence nor a real absence of that presence. Nothing gets born and nothing dies. Both, so to speak, are simply no-thing as that. Yet, and that's important, for no one.

Q: Hmm. So, what if I do get reborn after the body dies?

A: Then, this would be what apparently happens. Of course, no one would be reborn. It's pure speculation though.

Q: Isn't everything about the future pure speculation?

A: Yes, it is.

Q: So?

A: So what. There is no answer.

Make the prison nicer

Q: I was wondering about the seeking. Sometimes you hear that you should seek and sometimes you hear that it's exactly the seeking which is the hindrance. I don't know which way to go.

A: Well, the question you ask comes out of seeking. You assume even 'not seeking' to be a path that you could consciously walk. There is no question actually: Either there is the setup of 'I am' and seeking or there is no one. Then there is also no seeking.

Q: Ramana said that as long as there is someone, there has to be effort.

A: I would say it differently: As long as there is the illusion of being someone, there will be effort. Yet, the effort is illusory and doesn't lead anywhere. It's just part of the dream of 'I am'. The seeking drops automatically together with 'I am'.

Q: So, seeking doesn't lead anywhere. What do you think about the concept of at least making the prison more comfortable?

A: I don't really like it, because it sounds as if at least, you can do that. However, that's not the message. There is no person to choose anything. Exactly that's the dream: that there is a person who could consciously act according to its own will.

And yes, coming back to what you were asking in the beginning: The apparent me seems to survive on being active while it thinks that its efforts lead to fulfillment. That's the dream.

Q: But it's apparent.

A: Yes, it is. That's what apparently happens.

Q: So, it's better to stop seeking?

A: Well, who could do so? There is no one there. There is no seeker in seeking and there is no finder in liberation.

Q: But would you say that seeking is a hindrance?

A: It's not a hindrance. No one can choose to stop it. However, seeking is part of the dream of 'I am' and never leads out of that setup. The assumption that seeking leads somewhere is the misconception. In a way, it apparently confirms the 'me' in its existence and apparently only serves this existence. 'I am' is seeking in order to find something for itself. It has to survive in order to enjoy the fruits of its effort. Seen by the 'me', everything else would be madness.

Infant

Q: Andreas, Tony sometimes speaks of childlikeness. And Jesus also said that one should become like a child. What do you think of that?

A: Yes, that's true. However, regarding this message, it should actually say that you should become an infant. When one speaks about childlikeness, most people refer to the experience of a six- to nine-year-old. That was when their experience was unburdened by the life of an adult, yet, they were already there to experience it. Liberation, so to speak, would even go before experience. Becoming childlike would then mean that you should go where awareness was not born yet. Before experience itself, so to speak.

Q: But how would I do that? That's impossible for me.

A: Yes, exactly. It's impossible, simply because 'you' are awareness. 'You' is that which experiences itself as 'I was born, and I exist'. So, Jesus maybe meant that one "should" become like an infant.

Q: But, again, how would I do that?

A: Yes, you're right: You can't. First, because no awareness has ever been born. And secondly, because the whole experience of being awareness only consists of the experience of being something that has been born.

Q: What about deep sleep? Isn't it that liberation is like deep sleep?

A: Yes, in a way, it's like that. What can be compared to deep sleep is the absence of an experiencer. When there is the dream of 'me', there is the experience to be awake in the morning. Awareness wakes up in the morning saying "now I'm there".

Q: And that doesn't happen on your side?

A: No, it doesn't. There is no experience of there being something that wakes up. Waking up is what apparently happens, yet for no one.

Q: But to say this, doesn't it need awareness?

A: No, it doesn't. At least, not this self-awareness that lives in the experience of being something that's aware. There is apparent awareness for no one. Out of this apparent awareness, there is the apparent report that there apparently is waking up in the morning.

Q: That sounds complicated.

A: Yes, it does (laughs). You know, all of that is what apparently happens, just as it does on your side, whatever this may be or look like. It's real and unreal, whole and empty at the same time. No-thing appearing as some-thing, formlessness appearing as forms. But that's just words, they don't really mean or refer to anything.

Q: Does that mean that deep sleep, dream state and day consciousness are all the same?

A: Well, yes, in a way. They all are no-thing, however, for no one. No-thing apparently deep-sleeping, no-thing apparently dreaming and no-thing apparently waking. But to be precise: There is no experience of these three states being "all the same". There just is no one and nothing experiencing them to be different states. No one knows about there being deep sleep, as well as there is no one knowing that the waking state is something that's really different.

Q: Is there an experience of absence then?

A: No, there isn't. Presence and absence are not experienced.

Q: Is there awareness or consciousness at all?

A: Well, not really. Apparently, there is consciousness, and apparently there is awareness. Apparently, there is even presence. However, there is no experience of them being something real.

The barking dog

Q: U.G. once said: "I'm just a dog barking."

A: Yes, that's what I am. I'm just a dog barking. And this is what these talks are. This is what every conversation is: just barking dogs.

Q: But isn't it real? Don't you say something?

A: No, not at all. Speaking is what apparently happens, yet, it's devoid of reality and meaning. It may have apparent meaning, however, it's a dreamt meaning.

Q: So, you don't say anything?

A: No, not at all. But that applies to anyone and any conversation. No one is saying anything – it's just stories. It's all just barking.

Q: But why?

A: Because nothing true can be said. There is no real happening about which one could say something true. That reality doesn't exist in the first place. Apart from that, it's just what apparently happens. It's free-fall, yet, complete. I mean, barking dogs are just wonderful.

Q: And you don't say anything either?

A: Oh, no, it's all empty. All these things that I seem to talk about – awareness and liberation and the death of 'me' – don't exist. It's all empty talking. Yet, that's it. That's the beauty and the freedom of it. It's the beauty and the freedom of everything.

Living in liberation

Q: What can you say about living in liberation?

A: Well, not much actually. It's basically the same as everyone's life. However, just without that artificially added imaginary world that the 'me' seems to live in. There are so many assumptions in the 'me' world. The biggest one probably is the assumption that there is a purpose and a bigger goal in life, be it world peace or enlightenment or only "to live a happy life". Of course, all of these assumptions arise out of its sense of existence, yet, I think that this is the main difference. In many respects, I probably feel quite the same as you do, yet, there is no seeking happening in that. There is no one seeking for an additional absolute realization. This seeking is a total dream: assuming some weird state called enlightenment or fulfillment or happiness somewhere out there. Within the story, the 'me' puts all its energy in finding, becoming or being this ominous state that promises the fulfillment of all desires. Without that, there is still left what apparently happens: an apparently functioning body, apparently conscious, apparently aware with the apparent capability to think, feel and act, however, apparently freed from the illusion of there being a real spiritual self living in that body. There just is no such thing.

Q: Does this make you happier?

A: Yes and no. Of course, when there is no one, all the thoughts and feelings around that seeking drop – and, of course, they hold a huge potential for suffering: All those stories about 'me' and 'me and my life', about 'me not being happy' and all that stuff – that's the suffering. On the other hand, there is no escape from the body and daily life. So-called daily life is what apparently happens, and as I said, the body is apparently functioning, which means that it's capable of producing feelings and sensations. You can't leave that ... – which, by the way, is one of the attempts of the 'me': to leave this so-called day-to-day life and find a higher state where it can retreat to, just be and rest. That's what the spiritual aspirant longs for: an experienceable higher state.

Q: So, there is no higher state?

A: No, there isn't.

Q: There is no lower state either?

A: No, there isn't. There simply are no states. Living in states is nothing else than to live in experience – that's the dream: 'I experience something' or 'me and my life'.

Q: So, have you reached "perfect liberation"?

A: All there is, is perfect liberation. But 'you' can't have it. In the story, one could say that I died to it, however, this again may sound as if it had something to do with me. The surprise is that when "perfect liberation" happens, nothing happens. It never went away, so you can't gain it. The dilemma is that when we speak of "perfect liberation", the apparent me still thinks of an abstract state. It thinks of something personal that's separate from this simple, innocent and apparently worldly happening here. Yet, there isn't. This apparent happening here and now is the uncaused, timeless no-thing. There is no additional liberation in that, to that or from that. It's 'it'. It's whole and free already.

Q: Wow, it's really simple – but also very intense.

A: Yes, it's simple. It simply is. And yes, seen from the apparent perspective of 'me', it's intense. It's totality. This very ordinary happening is total. There is nothing parallel or extra. It's directly and uncompromisingly itself.

Q: So, is it always that intense?

A: Well, it's total, but also empty. It's totally itself, however, it's free from reality and meaning. It's cheerfully and delightfully light, unburdened by reality and the need to find anything else (e.g. purpose, sense, fulfillment and/or a higher state). Yet, for no one. That's just how it naturally is. It's not personal. It's not a state. It's not even an 'it'. It's just simply this apparent happening, which is naturally, simply and perfectly itself.

Healing & trauma

Q: Andreas, do you think that we have to resolve issues?

A: No, I don't think so. However, it's not about the issues. There just is no one who needs to do so. Leave the issues alone, and they will take care of themselves. Or rather: Leave yourself alone, and everything will take care of itself. There is no need to worry or bother about anything. The body will take care of itself.

Q: But what if there are any traumas or heavy stuff going on?

A: What then? Then that's what apparently happens. Seen by the 'me', the whole existence is an unresolved issue. The question about existence can't be answered at all. And the same applies to the questions about traumas. You know, what we talk about here, is so different from what the 'me' thinks what life is and what this apparent life is about. At the same time, this message isn't pointing to something else. It totally confirms that which apparently happens to be that which apparently happens. No shortcuts, no steps away, no denial. If what apparently happens is a traumatized body, that's what apparently happens. When there is no one, there is no one trying to work on the trauma, nevertheless, it seems as if exactly this may influence the healing of the trauma. And when I say "influence", it's actually coming from the wrong direction because, actually, it seems as if the trauma simply falls off when there is no one, simply by there being no one who has to be protected anymore. It seems as if the apparent me illusion is constantly influencing and reinforcing the traumatized body by its experience of being that body.

Since I died, more and more traumas are falling off. Simply, naturally and without making too much noise.

Q: Yet, would you say that you're still traumatized?

A: Yes, I would say so. However, if you see where I came from, there has been a lot of change. But what's also surprising is that these changes aren't real and don't bring about any real 'better'. In an absolutely great way, being traumatized is 'it', and apparently being freed from trauma is 'it' as well. Stunningly, it doesn't matter regarding the apparent wholeness of things.

Q: How do you think that it works?

A: Well, there just is no person which needs to be protected anymore. So, no one prevents the letting go from happening, we could say.

Q: Can this be life-changing?

A: Yes, of course. As most people build their lives around their needs and traumas, the falling off of the needs and traumas may also change the behavior of the apparent body. It doesn't matter, by the way, but yes, that's what seems to happen. Everything just seems to level out a bit. For no one, of course.

Q: Aha, okay. What did you mean when you said "where I came from"?

A: Well, when I died, what was left was a more or less traumatized body. And the death of 'me' doesn't mean that overnight all of the stored traumas dissolve. What dies is the illusion that there is an inner center, a core within the body which you are and which needs to hold it all together. In a way, it's the turnaround of the whole energy. While until then, the whole energy is based on need and survival – in simple terms: to keep and hold "your life" together – the energy after death is rather a movement of letting go. Instead of apparently keeping it all together, the energy is set free and is in a kind of a let go. Eventually, over the months and years, this apparent let go seems to permeate through the whole body and may cleanse it from traumas and stuff like that. However, there isn't a rule in that. It just is what apparently happens – or not. There is no meaning or truth in that, no development and no better or worse. And above all, there is neither someone doing it nor someone experiencing it.

Q: And when there are still traumas left over time?

A: Then that's what apparently happens. Look, this whole thing doesn't contain any real value. Being traumatized is as much wholeness as anything else. Seen from the me's perspective, that's a total miracle. You just are as you are, and I'm just as I am. Everything is naturally allowed.

Q: So, I don't have to first heal myself in order to become liberated?

A: That's what I say. The ideas about healing belong to the apparent 'me'. Yet, this whole "healing" thing doesn't contain any real value within itself. You know, it just isn't the issue. On the other hand, there just is no one who can become liberated. That's another idea. Liberation is the plain and simple death of the illusion to be someone. And that's just how death is: It doesn't ask for anything. It doesn't ask how much money you earned or if you paid all your taxes, and it doesn't ask either how much healing work you did. It just comes. The whole idea – and the experience – of being someone who is on a path is nothing but a dream. It just dissolves into blankness without any replacement. No success and no failures there – they are all part of the 'me' experience, which has no reality itself at all.

Q: Man, wow. All my life I was working on myself and trying to become a more peaceful person without noticing that I'm in a fight all the time.

A: Oh, yes, all the fighting for a person that doesn't exist in the first place. Living your life is what apparently happens. Healing – or no healing – is what apparently happens. Life apparently happens. It already is like that. It already is free. As it is. As you are. As I am.

Q: Oh, wow, that's wonderful.

A: Yes, it is. For no one.

Lingering ideas

Q: Andreas, I have another question. It's about an idea that I have been carrying around with me for several years. However, my life seems to move into a direction where I might not be able to follow that idea. I'm getting older and the chances to realize this seem to get less and less. What shall I do with that?

A: Well, I don't know. The main thing is that there is no one. And the main fear is that if you don't take action, you might miss an opportunity. Maybe *the* opportunity. However, I don't know. Who would be able to do something with it?!

Q: When we talked recently, I got a sense of the freedom that you speak about and the vastness of it.

A: Yes, 'what is' is boundless.

Q: Does it also include these ideas and maybe the feeling that I miss something?

A: Well, yes, of course. However, I assume that when there is no one, within a few years this idea will just fall away. It's quite possible that after liberation all kinds of ideas still linger around in the system. Usually, they drop off eventually.

Q: Does it have to be like that?

A: No, of course not. I mean, no one knows. You might go on living with that lingering idea for the rest of your life.

Q: Oh, no.

A: Well, in its own way, it would be what apparently happens and naturally okay. That's the surprise.

Q: Hmm. Sometimes it's as if there are two realities. Even when I'm fighting inside, there seems to be a peace underneath it.

A: These aren't really two realities. The amazing thing is that 'what is' is naturally whole. This 'being whole' doesn't really change 'what apparently happens'. There are still thoughts and feelings and you behaving in a certain way, yet, it's exactly that which is everything and which is whole and complete already. When I talk about liberation or freedom, I'm not referring to something which will still happen. I'm not referring to an additional aspect either. In that sense, 'what is' is just whole and, naturally, always has been. And if there are so-called old ideas lingering around feelings of regret, that's what apparently happens. And if it happens for the rest of your apparent life, it would be 'it', too. That's the freedom.

Q: Wow, that's truly immense. There are so many ideas around about becoming free.

A: Yes, that's right. However, there is no person to become free. Freedom is the natural reality, however, for no one. Liberation is the breakdown of the illusion that there is someone who is unfree and, eventually, the breakdown of all ideas and concepts that this apparent person was holding on to.

Q: Doesn't that happen all at once?

A: Not necessarily. You know, when the personal energy melts back into 'what is', so to say, you still have a conditioned and often neurotic organism – and a lot of the conditioning and neuroses that were built around that artificial need to protect the artificial person, are still in place and apparently playing out. Yet, eventually, they drop off naturally and organically after a while. This 'while' can last for years, of course.

Q: What can one do in order to do that?

A: Oh, nothing really. I mean, there is no one. It's not a process that could be consciously supported. Everybody who tells you so is back in the game of there being someone who could choose between right and wrong or between whatever. Usually, the people who refer to that experience themselves are someone and have the experience that they have to work on their path. Yet, liberation is effortless. 'What is' is effortlessly what it is.

Q: Can effort arise?

A: Not a real one. Yes, efforting seems to happen – effortlessly, of course.

Reverberation

Q: Andreas, I have a question which refers to the apparent time after liberation. Is it possible that after liberation there is some reverberation of personal stuff going on for a while? Like old habits, guilt feelings, shame or thinking?

A: Yes, that can happen. Many of these things can still linger on for a while. And when I say "for a while" this is quite relative. Some things can even linger on for months or years – traumas, for example. You know, in general, when the 'me' dies, there seems to be much more of the person left than the person has assumed it to be. That's simply because a lot of the functioning of the person has never been personal at all. Being responsible for thoughts, feelings, actions and reactions is part of the dream of 'I am'. So, a lot of this stuff apparently remains.

Q: Ah, okay. But how is the lingering on then?

A: Apparent liberation is the death of the illusion of there being a center. That center seems to nourish the functioning of the personal story by giving it attention. When that illusion of a center drops, there is no attention anymore that nourishes the thoughts and feelings of the personal story. Yet, the brain and hormone system still continue functioning. The character is still capable of thinking the same thoughts as before, and therefore it's still producing the same feelings. How fast this stuff desaturates depends on how deeply ingrained it is in the system, we could say.

Q: But does it matter to someone?

A: Oh, no, not at all. That's the funny thing when there is no one. Nothing matters. Apparently, personal stuff playing out is as much 'what apparently happens' than anything else. Nothing is better or worse than anything else. Therefore, nothing matters. That there is "personal stuff" is a story anyway.

Q: Wow. That sounds very natural.

A: Yes, of course. The apparent death of 'me' is neither unnatural nor superhuman. In its unique way, it's very organic and natural, like death is very organic and natural, even when it's sudden.

Dissociation

Q: Can you say something about dissociation? Some people think that you're just dissociated.

A: Yes, that's true. However, liberation has nothing to do with dissociation. Dissociation, in that sense, is a psychological function or rather: dysfunction (which is still some kind of functioning). Yet, I don't speak of the experience that there is no one or that the individual has to step back or deny itself. The individual may conclude that from what I seem to say, yet, it's absolutely not what I'm saying.

Q: I work in a psychiatric clinic – and people there often tell me that they don't feel themselves anymore, that everything is empty and doesn't make sense. That sounds quite like your words.

A: Yes, partly it sounds like my words, but actually, they refer to an experience. They refer to an experience of not being able to feel themselves. They refer to an experience of "nothing makes sense" – and, of course, then there is also suffering from that state. That's an apparently dissociated state. As a story, one could say, that liberation is quite the opposite of dissociation: It's the melting of the apparently dissociated 'me' with wholeness. Yes, there is no sense, no meaning. Yes, there is no one. Yes, everything is empty – and full, by the way – yet, for no one. And not as an experienced state. Many spiritual traditions actually teach some form of dissociation: There is a whole movement of people who suggest that you "just watch" or "simply be aware" as a way out of identification and the suffering that seems to come with it. That's actually promoting a dissociated state while claiming a connection to liberation. That's not what I speak about at all. I'm not promoting any state. States themselves are illusory in the first place. I don't suggest taking a certain standpoint. Any standpoint is illusory in the first place. There is nothing to escape from. No feeling, no emotion can threat you. Nothing can really harm you, simply because there is no one and nothing that could be harmed. It's all whole already. Look: That's the difference between this message and a teaching: With a teaching, there comes something that you're supposed to do, and there is some promise made. That's spinning around in the dream. This message doesn't claim or offer anything. As a side effect, it may become obvious that there isn't a problem with anything at all.

Excursions into science

A: As far as I know, the scientists haven't found an 'I' yet. And I assume that they will not find one either, namely because it's not there. And as far as I know, they can't even comprehend the idea of self-consciousness and bring it together with what they are finding out. Basically, they have no clue about what self-consciousness is. They don't even like their own theories about the 'I' consciousness, because they look insane to them, too. They seem to know quite something about the function of consciousness, but never connected with an 'I'. So, for modern science, there is no 'I' to be located anywhere. It's almost what this message is saying: There is no 'I'. Nevertheless, there are thoughts, feelings, functioning, very human and personal functioning, even consciousness – yet, for no one. It's amazing. It's really amazing.

Q: But, what do they do with it?

A: Well, of course, as there is probably still the experience of being a person for most scientists, it's just something that they can't comprehend by their own experience. In that sense, they still experience thoughts, feelings and consciousness as real and personal things.

Q: But they also find out that there is no reality.

A: That's true. However, they can't bring those results together. And still, it's a person that finds all that stuff out. It may be interesting and belief-shattering for these people, however, the person doesn't necessarily get killed by those apparent revelations. They just face what the spiritual seeker also faces: that there seem to be lots of revelations, information, conclusions, insights, understanding and knowledge – and in the end, they are useless. Neither of those does end the experience of separation as such. Neither of those brings about the one answer or the one conclusion. Of course, they can't bring about liberation, because they still take place within the setup of experience. All this understanding comes from an observing standpoint and happens for someone. No insight and no conclusion touch the experiencer itself. They just never touch it. Even finding out that there is no 'I' doesn't kill the 'I' – neither for the spiritual seeker after practicing "Who am I?" nor for the scientist who sees on his MRT that there is no 'I'.

Q: Hmm. What's liberation then?

A: In that sense, liberation is surrender, which is rather death than some holy state.

Q: Surrender?

A: Yes, surrender and letting go. Yet, I'm not talking about something that you can do. That would be the arrogance of the person which thinks that it can and has to consciously surrender. Liberation isn't dependent on you surrendering. We could say, oneness surrenders 'you', which means nothing else than that it kills you. And in killing 'you', it becomes obvious that there was no one to kill in the first place. It becomes obvious that there is no one who was bound to separation and had to become liberated. Separation never happened. In that sense, there was neither knowledge nor surrender.

Q: What becomes obvious?

A: That there is no 'me'. However, liberation isn't that obviousness. That obviousness isn't real and doesn't have any meaning. Liberation, however, is the end of the experience of being a separate entity. It's energetic and seen by the 'me', it seems very real. It's death and not some obviousness about some fact. There is no real obviousness, and there is nothing to see.

Q: There is nothing to see?

A: No, of course not. Oneness isn't a circumstance that can be seen. Again you're looking from a separate standpoint. However, there is no such thing. There will never be enlightenment in the sense of it being another experience. God will never be seen, simply because there is neither God nor some circumstance called "God". All there is, is this. 'This' means 'what apparently happens', or rather: No-thing as 'what's happening'.

Q: Yes, yes, I know. I know that this is all there is.

A: No, you don't know. How can you know what's unknowable?

Q: I don't know.

A: Me, too, I don't.

Criticism

Q: Andreas, you're often regarded as part of the Neo-Advaita scene which softens up the ancient and traditional teachings. You're accused of presenting some "enlightenment light" message and offering instant enlightenment. What do you think about that?

A: Not much actually. However, when you look a bit closer, you see that these people usually haven't really heard or were not really interested in what's being said here. Often, it's said that I claim "everyone is enlightened" and "you don't have to do anything in order to become enlightened". Yet, that isn't really what's being said here. What I say is that there is no one separate and no one to be enlightened or unenlightened. Of course, in that sense, there is no one who has to do something at all. Yet, doing may apparently happen – or not.

Q: They say that you make it too easy and that people like that simple stuff.

A: I don't say that it's easy. For the seeker, it's not easy at all. Seen by the seeker, it's impossible. The seeker will never get it. The seeker will never be free. Insofar, this message is quite heavy for the seeker. The ease is that what we speak about is already the case. 'What is' is naturally whole by simply being itself. 'What is' is absolutely at ease being what it is. There is no effort anywhere.

Q: But the seeker thinks that they have to do effort.

A: Yes, exactly. That's how the seeker lives. They discard the simplicity of 'what is' and live in the illusion that they have to arrive there. They overhear the simplicity of the message and turn it into something very difficult and complicated. Another interesting thing is that this message has been around in the so-called ancient times as well.

Q: Really?

A: Oh, yes, you can find it here and there. It's much rarer than all this spiritual stuff, however, it's there. And what these people talk about usually is the personal interpretation of this simple and pure message. That's the thing with any religion: The actual message degenerates into a footnote and becomes suffocated by the rituals, practices and traditions of the person. For the seeker, the path is much more important than the goal because being on a path reflects its experience. Therefore, the seeker has to discard a message that denies its existence and the need to practice.

Q: Another criticism is that you don't meet people from where they are. Is this message for everyone? Can it even be dangerous?

A: Well, theoretically it's for everyone. It doesn't say that you need any specific requirements. You don't have to have certain knowledge to face that. However, practically, it's only for those who are interested in it. And according to my experience, there are only a few people interested in that message. If you look at the numbers of people that are interested in that issue – compared to the numbers of people who are drawn to spiritual offers, for example –, you will see that they aren't many. There may be some who are around that message for a while, but the ones who aren't really ready – and I don't mean "ready" in a negative way or in terms of there being a path – lose interest very soon. They simply don't get what they are looking for. Their apparent needs just aren't recognized by me. They don't get the attention they long for. They don't get the entertainment they look for. They don't get highs of spiritual uplifting and so on. So, they go away after a while.

Q: What about it being dangerous?

A: Well, there as well, I don't see a real danger. Of course, this message can have a huge impact on people's apparent lives. And, of course, there are lots of misunderstandings around this message. However, in the long run, I don't know anyone who was more disturbed than they were before. Or anyone who robbed a bank because they mistook the message for something like "nothing matters". I mean, the whole "destruction" thing (which, potentially, sounds dangerous) refers to an illusion. What's also being pointed to – apparently – is wholeness itself. In a story-like sense, this is pointing to a healing that's already the case, which may sound very positive. Anyway, this message is totally neutral, so to say.

Q: There are people who say that you can't say this to people who aren't prepared.

A: Well, that's what I mean. My impression is that these people are simply not attracted to that message. There may be exceptions, yet, I actually don't see that happening.

Q: Some people also accuse you of giving a spiritual by-pass.

A: Yes, I know. I understand their impression, and I understand that they see it like that. However, my impression is that they never really followed what I say. Usually, that comes from *their* attempt to use this message as a spiritual by-pass and their experience that this doesn't work.

Q: Don't you say that there is nothing to seek?

A: Yes, of course, I do. But I don't say this to a person. I'm not trying to convince the person in order to create a better experience. But yes, of course, there is nothing to seek and nothing to find. Even all the so much honored people like Ramana Maharshi or Jesus point to this utter simplicity. I have no idea why this can be overheard so often. Well, me too, I overheard it (laughs). Most criticism that comes to my ears rather refers to what people think that I'm saying than to what's actually being said. And usually, I can "proof" that instantly. In a sense, this message is much closer to the ancient scriptures than many of these people criticizing me, respectively that message think. Yet, it's not coming from a learned knowledge. You know, often there is a lot of double standard going on: If Ramana never read any scriptures – or rather read the scriptures only years after his apparent awakening – that's okay. If Andreas Müller from Germany never did that, he must be a fraud because he hasn't read the scriptures. Not that I want to compare myself with Ramana. I have never met him and would not dare to speak up in his name. I mean, there are so many people out there claiming to be in Ramana's lineage who have neither met him nor were able to ask him if it's okay that they speak "in his name". Ignorant, that's what I think it is.

Q: You don't see yourself in Ramana's lineage?

A: Of course, I don't. As I said, I have never met him. I don't know what he was saying. Yes, there are these books – and there seem to be correlations, but, God, who the fuck knows!? Who of those self-appointed gurus have ever met him? And, by the way, look at what they say, what they "pass on": the most superficial of the superficial of Ramana's words. They turn it into their psychological and spiritual games. If you take him for real, that probably was not what he said.

Q: And how is he for you?

A: As I said, I don't know much about him. I don't care much about him. Not because I think anything specific about him. He is just not around and therefore can't play a big part in my life. I don't claim anything. I just say what I say, or rather: There are the words leaving my mouth that are leaving my mouth – and then we can discuss that.

Q: What about Tony Parsons?

A: Well, in the story, he told me that there is no one. However, why I heard it, I don't know. He is telling it to a lot of people (laughs).

Q: Do you refer to him in a kind of a lineage?

A: No, not really. It may look like that, and maybe it's like that, however, to speak of a lineage would absolutely contradict the whole message. Insofar, there is no experience of being a guru on his side, and there is no experience of having gotten anything, having reached anywhere or passing on anything on my side. You know, within the story, Tony was the one who told me, however, this whole thing is utterly impersonal. As I said, why I faded out and not so many others apparently, I don't know. And, you see, speaking like this already sounds as if something had happened at all. Again, we are missing the point. In the end, it had nothing to do with Tony, and it had nothing to do with me.

Q: So, does your message follow a tradition?

A: No, it doesn't. It comes from an utter directness. It seems as if you can find this message throughout history over and over again, yet, it never was coming from a tradition. The apparent person would love to squeeze it into a tradition with a path and special knowledge – and, above all, with something that you can and have to do. But what all these messages are trying to say is that there is no 'I' and nothing to get. This message can't be embedded into a system of beliefs, paths and hierarchy. In that sense, it speaks out directly what it means and therefore stands absolutely for itself. In the story, one could say: "Take it or leave it!" It doesn't leave any room for discussions – not because it claims to be right but because there isn't really anything to discuss. You know, that's the difference between a teaching and this direct communication: Within a teaching, the emphasis is on the path and of somehow "doing the right thing". The whole emphasis is on what you have to do in order to proceed on your path. In a teaching, there is hardly any emphasis on finally arriving there. But all the people that I would refer to as communicating this message state that there is no 'I', that there is nothing wrong and nothing to get. The apparent me simply doesn't want to hear this, therefore, it has to fight it. I know, just because some Indian guys said that a few decades or a few hundred years ago, it's easy to put them on a throne and assume that they were talking about a religion. Yet, they all stated that they were talking about something very natural and ordinary. Wholeness is that natural reality, which is nothing else than what seems to go on. There is nothing else. It's simple and plain and obvious.

Q: But I can't see it.

A: Yes, simply because there is nothing to see. Look, Ramana might have said: "Just give up the seeking." Exactly that's what liberation is: the end of seeking without finding anything. Yet, what's left is naturally whole. What's left is exactly this, yet, without the seeking for something else. That's it. Nothing has been found. Nothing has been additionally seen. It's just the end of the seeker.

Q: Hmm. How can the seeker end itself?

A: The seeker can't end itself, because there isn't even a seeker. The seeker doesn't exist.

Q: How can I make this become obvious?

A: You can't. I can't. Nobody can. Everybody is just helpless here. There is no way out and no way in. There is no path, because everything is already the goal.

Thanks to

Dorothea Gruß

Levin Sottru

Tony & Claire Parsons

My family

About Andreas

Andreas was born in 1979 in Ludwigsburg in Southern Germany. After taking drugs in his youth and seeking in spirituality afterwards, he met Tony Parsons in 2009.

"First, I was shocked. Though I had already known and experienced a lot, this was something new and unexpected. Suddenly, for no reason, I heard what Tony was saying, and soon it was undeniable: There is no one."

Since 2011, Andreas has been holding talks and intensives throughout the world.

www.thetimelesswonder.com

Also published in English:

No-thing – ungraspable freedom

ISBN: 9783839152928

Lightning Source UK Ltd.
Milton Keynes UK
UKHW020645270422
402137UK00009B/954

9 783735 757357